AF480668

LEAD YOURSELF FIRST

Return to Yourself and Lead from Alignment, Presence, and Truth

Liz Holtzinger

Lead Yourself First © Copyright 2025

Published by Wolf Media Group, an imprint of Present Tense, LLC

State College, Pennsylvania

All rights reserved. No part of this publication may be reproduced, distributed or transmitted in any form or by any means, including photocopying, recording, or other electronic or mechanical methods, without the prior written permission of the publisher, except in the case of brief quotations embodied in critical reviews and certain other noncommercial uses permitted by copyright law.

Although the author and publisher have made every effort to ensure that the information in this book was correct at press time, the author and publisher do not assume and hereby disclaim any liability to any party for any loss, damage, or disruption caused by errors or omissions, whether such errors or omissions result from negligence, accident, or any other cause.

Adherence to all applicable laws and regulations, including international, federal, state, and local governing professional licensing, business practices, advertising, and all other aspects of doing business in the US, Canada, or any other jurisdiction, is the sole responsibility of the reader and consumer.

Neither the author nor the publisher assumes any responsibility or liability whatsoever on behalf of the consumer or reader of this material. Any perceived slight of any individual or organization is purely unintentional.

The resources in this book are provided for informational purposes only and should not be used to replace the specialized training and professional judgment of a health care or mental health care professional.

Neither the author nor the publisher can be held responsible for the use of the information provided within this book. Please always consult a trained professional before making any decision regarding treatment of yourself or others.

For more information and contact information, visit lizholtzinger.com.

ISBN: 979-8-9941294-0-1 - Paperback
ISBN: 979-8-9941294-1-8 - Hardcover
ISBN: 979-8-9941294-6-3 - eBook
ISBN: 979-8-9941294-2-5 - Audiobook

BEFORE YOU BEGIN

If you want something to track your thoughts as you move through the book, the Leadership Compass is available as a companion page. It's simple, quick to use, and gives you plenty of space to write things down as you go.

Download it at: lizholtzinger.com

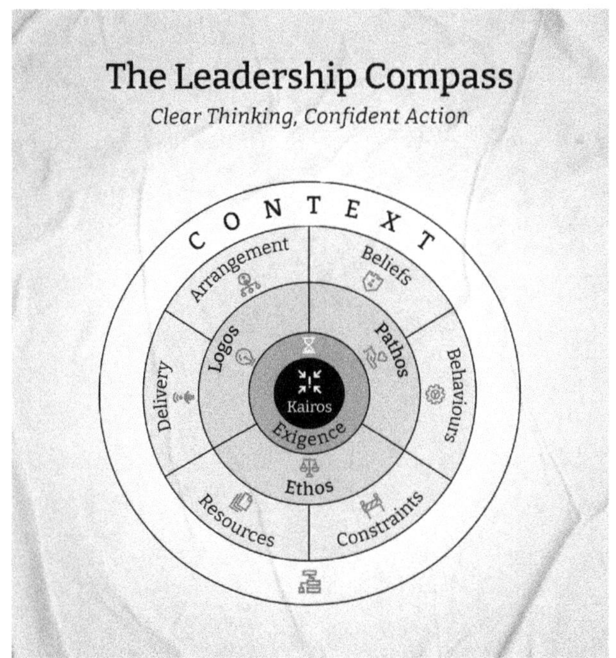

For GMFW, who loved me as I learned to lead myself home—and showed me what it means to lead from love, not fear.

CONTENTS

INTRODUCTION

Stop Outsourcing Your Clarity

*B*efore *the letter ever arrived, Clara had already learned the rules of her workplace—though none were written anywhere. The leader at the top operated by mood, not principle. Her power came from proximity: who she liked, who she didn't, who she could use to prove her own authority. When Clara spoke up or succeeded on her own terms, the leader found small ways to remind her who held control—public corrections, private slights, the kind of quiet undermining that leaves no evidence but takes a toll all the same.*

Clara wasn't new to leadership. She'd spent years helping other people find their voice, believing that truth and effort would always speak for themselves.

Then came the letter. Thick paper, university seal, formal tone. Unsatisfactory performance. Probation. No standards, no explanation, no precedent for what "probation" even meant—just a threat dressed up as procedure. The person who wrote it had never seen her work, never outlined expectations, never defined what "good" looked like. Still, the language was official, so it felt true.

Clara reported her supervisor's long pattern of behavior to HR. The letter was only the latest example, the last straw. They, in turn, called in an investigation, but, really, it wasn't one. The system did what systems do: It protected itself. "No problem found," they said, and filed it away. Clara went back to work, a little quieter this time.

For a long while, Clara led from that letter. Every decision was an attempt to prove she wasn't who they said she was. Every thought bent toward repairing a reputation she hadn't broken. The review became a mirror she didn't recognize but kept looking into anyway, searching for the version of herself they might finally approve of.

Similar to Clara, most of us are leading ourselves from lies and noise. We outsource clarity to media, bosses, cultural scripts, or the stories we've been telling ourselves for years. At work, that looks like waiting for our boss or a system to "make the call" instead of trusting our own judgment. In our personal life, it can sound like following cultural checklists—"I should have this job by 30, be married by 35"—without asking if they fit. And in politics, it's letting headlines or talking heads tell us what matters, then reacting and posting that reaction all over social media instead of discerning and...waiting to respond...or not respond at all.

When those stories don't resolve, people default to character attacks. In public, that means cheap shots—mocking a person's skin tone or age instead of engaging the issue. Internally, it sounds like: "I'm lazy," "I'm stupid,"

"I'll never get it right." These labels are easier than facing the harder truth: that maybe the problem isn't "them," but the unexamined patterns in us.

The result? People stay stuck in the same loops, blaming others or circumstances while repeating the very stories that keep them trapped.

Maybe you've felt it, too: the tug of doubt that says your success doesn't "count" unless it almost broke you. Or the quiet voice that asks if the story you're living even fits anymore. Or, as was true for Clara, the moment you realize the story you're in was written to keep you small.

This book isn't here to hand you another five-step plan or build atomic habits. It offers something sturdier: a compass. A way to orient yourself when the map is blank, the noise is loud, and the moment calls for a decision you can live with.

Built in the Classroom and Refined in Real Life

The framework that anchors this book was born in the classroom but refined in real life.

For years, I taught a model of communication, one that explained how we find meaning and move others to action. My students didn't know it came from Aristotle; they just knew it worked. I started noticing it worked outside the classroom too—in hard conversations, leadership decisions, and moments when the stakes were personal, not theoretical.

That model became what I now call the Leadership Compass, a way to read the moment you're in and choose how to respond with alignment, presence, and truth. It's not about winning. It's about understanding yourself in context and moving forward from that understanding. Because in every room, every pivot, every hard call, there's one person you must persuade before you can move at all: the one in the mirror.

With the Leadership Compass, you'll learn how to see a situation clearly, shift the story, and make choices for yourself from a position of self-leadership instead of survival.

What the Leadership Compass Is (and Isn't)

If you've ever felt like every tool is trying to fix you—or turn you into someone else—the Leadership Compass isn't that.

The Leadership Compass is not a goal-setting system. It won't tell you how to scale, launch, optimize, or monetize.

It's a clarity tool designed to help you reconnect with what's already true before you make your next move. It's built for leaders, creatives, and changemakers navigating moments of transition, misalignment, or quiet revolt. The Leadership Compass helps you:

- Re-anchor to your own values, vision, and voice.
- Examine what systems you've been shaped by and whether they still serve you.

- Identify how you show up under pressure (and what parts of you go quiet).

- Make strategic decisions from sovereignty—my preferred term for "self-leadership"—not survival.

- Help you see what influences you, what drives you, and how to move forward in a way that actually fits.

Your Reading Journey: The Book's Setup

The book unfolds in the following three parts:

Part 1: The Stories We Inherit

Before we can lead ourselves, we have to see the stories we're leading from. Part 1 explores the narratives we inherit about worth, work, and what it means to "earn" our place and how they quietly shape our choices. Through childhood memories, family legacies, and early self-doubt, Part 1 reveals how clarity begins not by fixing ourselves, but by facing the unexamined stories we've been living inside. By the end of this section, you'll begin to recognize the patterns that have shaped your leadership and consider loosening their hold.

Part 2: The Compass in Motion

Once we start recognizing our stories, we can begin to reorient. Part 2 introduces the Leadership Compass in action: how to read the room, reclaim your voice, and navigate emotion without being ruled by it. Through lessons on context, ethos, pathos, logos, exigence, and kairos, we see how leadership begins with awareness and alignment, not authority, and how we can learn to move through life with intention instead of reaction. Here, you'll learn to translate awareness into movement: how to use discernment, timing, and presence to lead yourself forward.

Part 3: Leading from Wholeness

Clarity is only powerful when it becomes practice. The final section brings the Leadership Compass full circle, showing how sovereignty (as mentioned, in this book sovereignty means self-leadership) looks in real life: the way we decide, communicate, rest, and rebuild. This is where self-leadership stops being theory and becomes a lived rhythm, guiding us back to trust, to truth, and to home within ourselves. By the close of the book, you'll understand how to sustain alignment—not as an outcome to achieve, but as a way to live.

The LYF of Your Choosing

This book's title, *Lead Yourself First,* came first—before I realized what it spelled if I turned it into an acronym: LYF. Life. Which felt fitting. Because this isn't just a book about leadership as a role or skill. It's about the life you choose to lead when you stop outsourcing clarity and start listening inward.

With this said, let's return to Clara, the woman tracing the embossed letterhead, reading the word *unsatisfactory,* and trying to decide what it said about her. For a long time, she believed every word. She built her days around repairing a reputation someone else had invented.

A confession: Clara is me. I believed the story about my work performance because it came with a seal and a signature. But clarity doesn't live on letterhead.

The story of me losing and regaining my own clarity isn't separate from this book. It's the reason for it. Because when you've been made to doubt your own voice long enough, the hardest person to persuade is yourself. Throughout this book, I'll regularly touch on my own story so you can see how I evolved from doubt to clarity in my life as a whole. Talk about the *ultimate transformation* and one that—with Leadership Compass and your own dedication and self-love—you, too, will come to embody.

At its root, this book is about persuasion, but not the external kind. The internal kind. The kind that says: "You already know. You already are. You can trust what's true."

This book doesn't promise that everything will fall into place. It's not a guarantee of wins or a roadmap to ringing the bell. And it's certainly not a prerequisite for doing big things with your life.

But coming home to yourself is a foundation.

Really, it is *the* foundation.

Once you know how to return to yourself—how to anchor, listen, and believe—you stop outsourcing your clarity. You stop wobbling so hard every time the world gets loud. The decisions you make come from a grounded place, not a panicked one.

And that's where the LYF you were meant to live finally begins.

If, along the way, you find yourself wanting to keep exploring these ideas—to keep unfolding what leadership and clarity look like in real time—I'd love to continue the conversation with you. You can join me on *Unfold*, my Substack community (https://lholtzinger.substack.com/), where these reflections take living shape.

For those who feel called to bring this work into their own rooms, teams, or stages, I now speak and teach on the Leadership Compass and the art of leading from wholeness. Because clarity isn't a one-time revelation. It's a rhythm we return to, together.

Every journey toward clarity starts with a reckoning—with the voices, lessons, and expectations that shaped us. Before we learn to steer, we have to see what's been steering us. That's where our work begins.

PART 1
The Stories We Inherit

Every one of us is carrying a story that taught us how to survive, but that same story may be keeping us from leading and living more fully. Some of those stories were whispered to us through family, faith, or culture; others we wrote on stone tablets in our hearts in moments of fear, failure, or longing. They're not bad stories. They just stopped fitting. And before we can lead ourselves with clarity, we have to name the stories that trained us to doubt ourselves. This first part begins there—with the stories we inherited, the voices we believed, and the quiet work of remembering who we were before we forgot. It's the same invitation Tinkerbell gives to Peter Pan in *Hook*: "Don't you know who you are?" The question isn't about nostalgia. It's about recognition.

CHAPTER 1

Did You Let Me Win?

A Sovereign Take on "Earning" It

I grew up in a little town called Milesburg, Pennsylvania. We lived in a cozy three-bedroom home with a really cool den and acres of land that felt endless to me as a kid. The driveway wound up and down a big hill, and after it rained, I'd go "fish" with broken tree sticks in the driveway's puddles. It was a place made for imagination, for exploring, for feeling safe and sound.

Inside, Mom fed us three square meals a day and avoided offering unneeded snacks. My older sister, my father, and I played board games—Sorry, Monopoly, Chutes and Ladders—on the living room floor. And when we played, it was quiet, focused, each of us contemplating over how to win the game.

Except...

I lost. A lot.

I remember furrowing my brow. I wouldn't cry over losing, I'd just sit there and stew and be pissed off—not because anyone cheated, nor because Dad or Jen had won, but because I couldn't figure out how to win. Some kids might throw a fit or storm off. I didn't. I just sat there, seething inside, thinking: "I'm never going to get this, am I?"

Then, one day, I won.

And instead of celebrating, I asked: "Did you let me win?"

Because that "win" felt...suspect. It had never happened before. And I didn't trust it.

That question, it turns out, would become a kind of ghost. It still lingers. It still visits. It's the voice that says: "Did this happen because I earned it... or because someone gave it to me?"

Even at five, I had developed not just a "sore loser" complex—but a "suspicious winner" complex too, what some people call "imposter's syndrome."

I didn't want dumb luck. I didn't want a pity move. I didn't want someone to go easy on me because I was the youngest or the least skilled. What I wanted was to *know* I had caused the win. That I had figured it out. Played the strategy. Made the right moves. Earned it.

Otherwise? It didn't count.

And looking back now—blonde curls, quiet voice, deep dimples—I can see how painfully naive I was. Not just in the surface way, but in the aching, break-your-heart way that comes from watching a little girl try so hard to be smart enough; to be good enough; to *deserve it*—whatever "it" even was.

She didn't know her brain wasn't done forming. She just knew that losing felt bad and winning felt suspicious. And somehow, she decided that to matter, the win had to be earned.

That story—it stuck. And it's an all-too-common story that's stuck for so many others as well.

Maybe you've carried it, too—the quiet belief that everything worth having must be hard-won. That if it comes easily, it's probably a fluke. Maybe you've caught yourself replaying old messages: *Work harder. Prove it. Earn your keep.* Maybe you've brushed off praise or minimized a success, worried that someone might discover you didn't quite deserve it.

If so, then you know the story I'm talking about—the one that keeps us striving long after we've already arrived, the one that makes rest feel risky and enoughness feel unearned. The story that keeps us outsourcing our clarity instead of trusting what's already true.

But maybe this is where that story can start to loosen—where we can stop proving and start leading ourselves home.

When we're young, stories like that feel harmless—quirks of personality, small lessons about effort and reward. But over time, they harden. They become invisible compasses—quietly steering how we measure our worth, our work, even our belonging. For some, the needle points toward constant proving: more hours, more output, more evidence that you've earned your place. For others, it swings toward hesitation, a fear of stepping forward until someone else declares you ready. Either way, the direction is the same: outward.

This is where you turn the compass inward. To see where your definitions of "earning it" still pull you off course. To question the standards guiding your choices and name which ones are truly yours and which were borrowed from someone else's map. Sovereignty begins here: when you stop letting inherited stories orient you, and reclaim the authority to decide what counts, what matters, and what's true.

The Impact of Legacy

My last name is Holtzinger. In the city where I grew up—Altoona, Pennsylvania—that meant something.

We moved there when I was six, leaving behind our first home in tiny Milesburg. Altoona became what I consider my *true* hometown. And in that place, our family name carried weight.

My family owned and published the local newspaper. My grandfather, Ted, was the grandson of the founder and became publisher, eventually passing the torch to my Aunt Marge, before it landed in my father's hands. The paper felt like part of the town's pulse—and so did our name.

People thought we were rich. They assumed ownership meant wealth, power, and privilege.

People thought we had it easy because we "owned" something. They didn't see how my mother pinched pennies and avoided snacks because snacks cost too much money, money we didn't have. If an item wasn't necessary or wasn't "on sale," my mother wasn't buying it because we couldn't afford to waste a single dollar. They didn't see how hard my dad worked; how seriously he took the family legacy; how much responsibility he held—for his employees, for the community, for our family.

As a kid, I didn't carry that weight. But I felt the ripple.

My dad was a great dad, deeply present in spirit and love, but often pulled away by duty. My mom—quiet, steady, and practical—held the center. She made sure our home worked, that we had what we needed, that the small things stayed intact when the big things around us were demanding. She stretched every dollar, carried the daily responsibilities without fanfare, and created a kind of stability that only becomes obvious once you're old enough to understand what it took.

And the town?

It looked at me as if I'd already won. Like my last name itself should count for something.

But I didn't want the *appearance* of winning. I wanted the *experience* of earning.

I didn't want the name to do the heavy lifting. I wanted to be measured as a standalone person. Not a "Holtzinger."

Looking back, I probably overcorrected. I stayed under the radar. I deflected attention. I tried to prove that whatever I got, I got on my own.

Still, advantages found me.

I was tested early and recommended for the gifted program. My parents declined. They were worried I'd feel even more "othered" than I already did.

But in junior high, there was no opting out. My test scores spoke for themselves, and I was placed on the gifted track. And that word—*gifted*—still makes me wince. Because it didn't feel like a win. It felt like something I'd been handed. Something I hadn't earned but had inherited by virtue of my name, my environment, my proximity to achievement. It felt just like that board game win: something I wasn't sure I'd figured out, something I feared had been decided for me, not by me.

Even when the outcome was real—my score, my placement, my abilities—I doubted it. Because if I was so smart—*why was I still losing at Monopoly?*

And on the rare occasion that I did win, why was I still doubting the win?

Why did I still feel like I hadn't earned that which came easily?

It's strange how fast a story forms: that if something came through connection, or ease, or luck, it didn't count; that the only wins that mattered were the ones I had to bleed for.

That story?

It stayed with me, too.

And I am not alone in this.

Maybe you've felt it, too—the pressure of a name, a role, a reputation you didn't exactly choose but were expected to uphold. Maybe your version isn't a family business but a family expectation: to be the achiever, the caretaker, or the one who keeps it all together. We all inherit stories about what it means to be "worthy," "successful," or "good." They begin as gifts—a sense of belonging, direction, pride—but can quietly become cages.

This is where self-leadership begins: in noticing whose definition of "earning it" we're living by. The Leadership Compass helps us locate those inherited coordinates and decide whether they still point toward truth—or just tradition. Because sovereignty isn't rebellion for rebellion's sake; it's the steady, conscious act of charting your own course when the world has already shown you *a* way. Remember that—the world has shown you *a* way; not *the* way.

Spot the Pattern

That board game moment didn't stay in childhood. It just got better at disguising itself. The same question—"Did you let me win?"—didn't always emerge so clearly. But its energy? It still showed up.

It showed up when someone chose me for a high-stakes project, and I wondered if they chose me "just to be nice."

It showed up when someone close to me implied that any success I had over the course of my career was the result of someone else "giving it" to me.

It showed up when something came easily, and instead of trusting it, I quietly discredited it.

And when I have worked hard—when I *really* grind myself into a fine pulp—it feels okay to win. When I received a prestigious teaching award, I didn't doubt it for a second. Because I had worked my ass off. And that's what it takes to win awards, right?

But anything that didn't come with exhaustion, sacrifice, or visible sweat? That's when my alter ego, SWINI—*She Who Is Never Impressed*—comes out to play. She's subtle, but she's sharp. "Cute," she'll sneer, when I pause to celebrate a small win, "but it doesn't count unless it rings the bell."

Organizational psychologist Adam Grant once posted on his social media that "self-doubt can be a sign of integrity."[1] I love that reframe. It's elegant. Empathetic. It gives high achievers permission to feel uncertain without immediately pathologizing it.

But let's be honest—some of us (me) have taken that to professional levels. We don't just experience self-doubt. We *inhabit* it. We turn it into an ethic. A way to earn our place at the table by questioning whether we belong there at all.

And while I admire Grant's clarity—and share his academic wiring—I know this pattern doesn't always signal integrity. Sometimes, it signals injury. A belief so deep-rooted it becomes reflex: If it didn't cost you something, it doesn't count.

She Who Is Never Impressed is that reflex. She distrusts anything that doesn't feel hard. She discredits what comes naturally. She's the one who whispers, "Nice try, but it doesn't count unless it damn near broke you." She's not wise. She's just tired. She's tired because she's been keeping watch for decades—through breakdowns, betrayals, silences, shame; through the years when I went quiet about what hurt and loud about what I could achieve instead.

She's not irrational. She just doesn't know *the war is over.* Her voice has stolen more joy than any failure ever could.

And perhaps the most heartbreaking part is realizing how often I've stood on a mountaintop, accomplishment in hand, and said, "It's no big deal."

Even when it absolutely was.

Maybe you, like so many others, can relate.

If so, it's time to reclaim leadership over our own lives.

Reclaim the Lead

Self-leadership isn't ego. It isn't dominance. It's not about becoming untouchable, invincible, or above the mess.

It's about becoming *a source.*

Not the controller of everything—but the one who stops outsourcing their clarity; who roots themselves in something deeper—truth, discernment, wholeness—and no longer hands their power to the loudest voice in the room.

There's a part of me that's always known how to lead. But I spent too long believing that kind of knowing had to come from someone else.

I gave that power away—to institutions that didn't know how to hold me; to students I tried too hard to rescue; to systems and people who didn't know how to carry what I carry and never asked if I needed help; and to "experts" who promised clarity but couldn't meet my depth, who praised the container but ignored the contents and still expected payment in full.

They're not blameless. But they're not the ones who dropped the boundary. I did. I'm the one who led from unexamined stories.

When I talk about leading our own selves, I'm referring to a sovereignty, a self-leadership, that:

- recognizes who we are and what we're actually capable of carrying.
- knows when to lift, when to release, and when to let others hold their own weight.
- doesn't conform to what the masses want us to do.
- doesn't ask for consensus.

Self-leadership shows up in the smallest corners of our lives:

- When and how we care for ourselves.
- When and how we tend to the anchors of our health, our rest, our rituals.
- When and how we don't let social media spin us into a frenzy of comparison or false urgency.

- When our inner knowing sends up a flare and asks, "Is this for you...or against you?" and we actually stop and listen.

Self-leadership lives in the way we manage our money. We don't passively let it run in the background anymore. We pay attention to it. We see it. We learn about it and act accordingly.

Self-leadership allows us to reclaim our workday. I still sometimes set the bar way too high; I still do more than expected but no longer at the cost of my body, my peace, or my soul.

Sovereignty is what self-leadership looks like. It's not loud. It's not flashy. It's not a TED Talk. It's choosing not to abandon ourselves in the name of being impressive. It's catching the moment She Who Is Never Impressed starts to stir and choosing to not hand her the mic.

That's how I win *now.*

That's how you can win *now* too.

Frequently. Daily, even.

Wins aren't awards. They aren't the applause or likes on a social media post. They are not the perception.

The win is knowing when to stay, when to walk away, and when to wait for more information. The win is examining the stories you carry and picking and choosing which ones stay and which can be released. The win is saying, "I don't need to bleed to believe myself anymore." The win is coming home to your own instincts and knowing you can trust yourself.

Sovereignty says, "I'm already worth celebrating. And I don't need to wait for someone else to name it first."

Own the Win

I don't ask that question anymore: "Did you let me win?" Because I know the answer now. No one handed me this life. No one scripted the clarity. No one softened the path or slipped me the strategy.

I earned it.

I grieved it.

I excavated it.

I had to dig myself out—from the rubble of a life that looked fine from the outside but buried me underneath its weight. I didn't "assemble" this next version of me.

I *unburied* her. I stopped outsourcing my worth; stopped performing for approval I didn't need; stopped asking other people to name what I already knew.

And I started listening inward: to the instincts that had been there all along; to the clarity that doesn't shout, but never lies; to the version of me who no longer waits to be crowned.

I don't win by chance.

I don't win by pity.

I don't win because someone lets me.

I win because I led myself home. To me.

You can do the same. This book provides the compass.

Chart the Way Forward

This is the very beginning of the story. It's what sovereignty sounds like when it finally lands. *Lead Yourself First* is a guide to what it *means* to lead yourself first—not in theory, but in motion. Action. Real life in real time.

If you've been reading this and wondering how to move from here to there—from the noise of everyone else's expectations to the quiet clarity of your own—this book will point toward your inner knowing and show you how to *trust* it and steady yourself in it.

LYF is not about "finding your purpose."

LYF is about coming back to the one who never left and making decisions from a place that's *already whole.*

If you've ever felt like your success doesn't "count"...

If you've ever doubted your wins because they didn't come with bruises...

If you're ready to lead from clarity—not exhaustion...

LYF is *for you.*

A LYF of self-leadership doesn't begin with strategy; it begins with *memory.* To understand how to lead yourself forward, you first have to find your way back. Let's dig in...

CHAPTER 2

The Way Back

Coming Home to Yourself

You already know the ghost: the little child who didn't trust the good things; who needed their wins to come with blood, or they didn't count; who carried the ache of *almost believing* they were enough—if only they could prove it.

Here's the part of their story that came first, the part that didn't need to be earned because some stories don't begin with pain. Some begin with grass-stained knees.

Before I knew words like *ambition* or *achievement*, I knew how to fly—legs pumping hard on the backyard swing set, sneakers kicking toward the sky, certain I could reach it. Not performing. Not trying. Not acting for a five-second reel to post on social media. Just...Being.

And for a while, that was enough.

I had a dad who worked hard and played even harder with his beloved daughters, crouching his tall six-foot-four body to the floor, sitting cross-legged, and playing board games with us like it mattered. I had a mom who made sure we were well-rested and with bodies healthy and nourished—always. No fuss. And I had a sister whom I admired and wanted to be just like and who made me laugh.

Maybe you remember a moment like that, too—the kind that felt effortless, when joy arrived without needing to be earned. Maybe it was a backyard, a ballfield, a classroom, or a kitchen table. You didn't have to prove yourself to belong there; you just did. That's the place this book asks you to return to—not as an escape from the world, but as a reminder of the wholeness that's always been yours to lead from. Before you learned to chase, you already knew how to trust.

My First Definition of "Safe"

Just inside the front of the house, past the porch and tucked beneath the trees, was the den—a dark, tree-shaded alcove tucked into our house like a secret—where the TV lived. Where my sister and I would sit on the hearth of the fireplace, close, as the screen flickered and the world slowed down.

We watched *Little House on the Prairie* and *The Waltons*—stories full of simpler times and strong families and quiet evenings that looked a lot like ours.

And it just felt so...safe.

The den didn't ask me to be impressive; it didn't expect brilliance.

It just held us. That room knew how to keep us close—without performance, without noise. Just a family, two sisters, a warm hearth, and a kind of peace I didn't yet know how to name.

Sometimes, mostly when Mom wasn't looking, we'd ride our bed pillows like sleds down the carpeted stairs—squealing, crashing, laughing—joy in motion, rule-breaking in its gentlest form.

Even mischief felt safe.

And then there were the make-believe games—still full of joy, just a different kind. At our babysitter Kate's house, we played church, just the three of us—Kate, my sister Jen, and me. Kate was the organist at our actual church, the one we attended every Sunday, and when we played church, she'd sit at the piano in her home and accompany our make-believe service. Jen and I took turns preaching. I couldn't read yet, but I'd open the Bible in my lap and pretend to read scripture—sounding out made-up verses with all the seriousness I could muster.

We sang. We laughed. We believed.

It was pretend, yes—but not fake. Something sacred, even in play.

Going to Kate's was always a treat, and we didn't want to leave.

When our parents came to pick us up, we'd lie still on the couch, eyes clenched shut, pretending to be asleep, hoping they'd find it rude to wake us and, instead, let us stay. We didn't realize we were small enough to be carried.

We were small enough to be carried.

So they lifted us...Back to the car. Back to our den. Back to the place where we were safest. Back to the people who loved us most. We didn't need to stay where joy was happening. Joy would follow us home.

And love would always come get us, whether we were playing, pretending, or asleep.

Our parents did the carrying then. They lifted us from playtime to bedtime, from Kate's couch to our own beds—because they knew where we belonged. Because they wanted us safe. Because love, at its best, doesn't wait for you to ask for safety.

Maybe your version of safety didn't look like mine. Maybe it came from a friend's house, a grandparent's hug, the quiet of a library, or the steadiness of your own imagination. Or maybe you never had a place that felt safe at all, and the idea still feels far away. But even then, there's a part of you that remembers what it means to rest, to breathe, to belong. That memory, real or imagined, isn't a luxury; it's a *landmark*. It's proof that *safety can live inside you*, even if you have to rediscover it now. Learning to lead yourself begins here—with the belief that you can offer yourself the care you once waited for.

When We Forgot the Way

Still, even the surest landmarks can fade over time. Life tugs us forward, and somewhere along the way, we start to forget the way back.

We got taller. And busier. We took some hard knocks. Got sharper with ourselves. We learned words like *pressure* and *performance*. We stopped needing to be carried.

Somewhere along the way, we forgot how to "come home" on our own. We traded our joy for strategy. We traded rest for relevance. We started measuring our worth in output, outcomes, and other people's approval. And we wandered.

Not because we failed, but because that's what grown-ups do.

The Leadership Compass shows us how we find our way back. Not to childhood, exactly; not to nostalgia—but to the truest part of ourselves that never left.

The Leadership Compass isn't a return to being taken care of. The Leadership Compass points you toward the kind of care you can give to *yourself.* It helps you lift up what matters and set down what doesn't.

It helps you remember how peace feels, so you can choose it again. It helps you carry yourself back to the swing set, back to the den, back to joy that doesn't need to be earned and the clarity that never once abandoned you.

And the girl on the hearth? She still believes the world is not a scary place; that it is *for* her—not against her. She knows she doesn't have to pump her legs so high anymore, past the danger zone, to prove she belongs in motion. She knows the swing set won't tip. She trusts the ground now. She knows she is surrounded; held by the people who matter.

The other stuff? It's not her voice. It's just noise.

What if you could return to *your* voice, not the loud one of others? The true one. The one who's been here the whole time, waiting for you to come home. A stripping-away of what doesn't fit. A reclamation of what's always worked. A deeper trust in the basics that hold you.

What if you could come back to yourself—quietly, clearly, and without performance? What if you could remember that you don't have to earn your way into enoughness?

You only have to believe you're enough—and live like you do.

Coming home to yourself is one thing. Learning to steady there—to see yourself clearly when the world starts shouting again—is another. That's where we'll turn next.

CHAPTER 3

Mirror, Mirror on the Wall

You Don't Need a Plan; You Need a Mirror

"Mirror, mirror on the wall..."

We were taught to ask, "Who's the fairest of them all?" But the real question I often find myself asking when I look in the mirror is this—"Who do you think you are?" —and it's not asked kindly. It doesn't come from confidence or curiosity. It comes from a place of doubt. Of judgment. A voice that doesn't believe I belong in the room. It's a voice that doesn't want an answer so much as it wants to shame me for even asking the question at all.

For years, I ran on the logic of effort. If I could just show up harder, stay later, push through—eventually everything would click. Eventually, someone (me?!?) would call it "success," and I could finally rest. But it didn't work like that. I crossed finish lines and still felt unfinished. I checked the boxes and still felt lost. The criticism got louder just as my own voice got quieter. And somewhere in all of that—

achievement, exhaustion, high-functioning doubt—I started asking a better question, and I started asking it kindly: "Who are you?"

The book's Leadership Compass doesn't tell you where to go. It shows you where and who you already are. It will show you who you are; it will see you *in fairness*.

Because when that voice inside sneers (Remember mine?!? SWINI—She Who Is Never Impressed!), "Who do you think you are?" The Leadership Compass doesn't answer with shame. It doesn't posture. It doesn't sell us a rebrand. It holds up something steadier.

It reflects what's already there: the values we live by, even when no one's looking; the quiet boundaries we've drawn without applause; the inner knowing we've carried all along, beneath the noise.

The Leadership Compass doesn't yell over the voice of doubt. It just refuses to lie. And in that way, it teaches us to do the same.

Your Problem Isn't a Lack of Direction. It's Too Many Directions.

I used to think I just needed a better system—maybe a day planner, a routine, or a five-year plan. Maybe I just needed to set the right goals—hit the right milestones—and then I'd feel like I was winning.

And to be fair, some of that helped. It gave me structure. But it didn't give me clarity. Because those goals weren't really about me. They were about achievement. Approval. Proof.

I've since learned that goals *can* help, but only when they're grounded in who you actually are, not just what someone else wants from you.

I wasn't lost. I was drowning in too many directions, each one promising to fix the chaos but only adding to the noise. And I don't think I'm alone in this.

There's no shortage of advice out there: Optimize your time. Find your niche. Build your brand. Lean in. Pull back. Hustle smart. Rest hard. Be visible. Be quiet. Stay grateful. Ask for more.

It's no wonder we're tired.

Most of us aren't flailing. We're fragmented, tugged in a dozen directions by strategies that promise clarity, but only deliver more noise. And for high achievers especially, this can feel like a personal failure. We're not just exhausted—we're ashamed that we still don't feel aligned after everything we've done "right." You start to wonder, "Maybe I'm the problem. Maybe I'm just not built for this. Maybe clarity isn't available to someone like me."

But here's what I want to offer—what I've lived: It's not that you're lost. It's that your internal compass has been drowned out by everyone else's.

At some point, I stopped reaching for another framework. I stopped asking someone else to chart the way. I hesitate reading some popular books like James Clear's *Atomic Habits* and Mel Robbins' *Let Them*. Why? Because every well-intended, advice-providing "influencer" I followed led me further away from myself.

That's when the Leadership Compass emerged. A way to return to myself. A way to name what I already knew. A way to feel the difference between momentum and misalignment.

The Leadership Compass isn't about where you're going. It's about where you're leading from.

The Mirror Moment

There wasn't one dramatic moment. It was a slow unraveling: meetings where ideas were buried under fear; proposals that never moved forward unless they came with a spreadsheet of guarantees; a constant undertow of hesitation—masked as diligence—that made everything feel heavier than it needed to be.

At first, I thought it was just the environment. Then I thought it was me. I over-functioned. I adapted. I softened my language. I changed how I showed up—literally. I wore athleisure and stopped wearing makeup, because that's how my work-from-home boss showed up. And I knew the rules: Play to the crowd, blend in, don't outshine. It grated against every professional instinct I had. Working from home is no excuse for abandoning presence. Dressing down wasn't about comfort—it was about conformity. And in that environment, *polish* was read as *provocation*.

So I toned it down. I told myself that the compensation made it worth it.

But slowly, I was shrinking inside my own body, mind, and soul.

That's the dissonance no one prepares you for: when the paycheck feels like security, but it costs you clarity. When you keep saying yes because it seems like a deposit—while your spirit is being slowly overdrawn, one quiet withdrawal at a time.

Eventually, I stopped reaching for more. Not out of defeat—but out of clarity. I saw what was true: I was performing leadership in a place that had no room for it. And no amount of praise, professionalism, or polish could close that gap.

Leaving wasn't easy. There was grief. There was the ache of untapped potential and relationships I still cared about. But when I finally stepped away, it felt like air rushing into a room that had been sealed shut. That was the mirror moment. The day I stopped looking for a leader to believe in me—and started believing in myself.

What came next wasn't a plan. It was a practice. I didn't pivot. I returned to what I knew before I learned to doubt it.

Most of us don't need a pivot. We need a pause. A chance to ask, "Am I where I am meant to be, or am I just where I happened to land?"

The Hardest Part? Applying It in Real Time

The truth is, even when you know what the Leadership Compass is reflecting, it's hard to obey it. There was that one time I returned a phone call I knew I shouldn't have—because pathos made me do it (it's okay if you don't know what "pathos" means yet; I'll explain it in detail later). My gut told me not to re-engage. But I let someone else's voice override my own and convinced myself, "Maybe just this once…"

It wasn't just a bad call. It was a small betrayal of what I already knew.

Afterward, the Leadership Compass didn't shame me, not like SWINI would have. It just reflected what I already knew: "I don't want to spend my energy in places—or with people—that don't feel aligned anymore."

And that's the work: not knowing better—*choosing* better.

The Five Anchors of the Compass

Unlike a traditional compass that points to cardinal directions, the Leadership Compass offers five points of inward reflection: (1) context, (2) ethos, (3) pathos, (4) logos, and (5) exigence and kairos. And yes—if you're wondering why some of these sound like unfamiliar terms, it's because they come from Aristotle's rhetorical tradition. I promise I'm not trying to be fancy. These are just ancient tools made relevant again. The anchors aren't destinations. They're orientations—each one a different lens through which to understand where you are, what you carry, and how you move.

Each section of the Leadership Compass is a prompt, really—a reflective space mapped to one of five foundational concepts:

1. Context—an examination of your setting

First, locate yourself. See the systems, settings, and dynamics shaping your decisions. Notice what expands your possibilities and what constrains your clarity.

2. Ethos—an examination of the self

Ethos is who you are when no one's watching. It's the integrity between word and action, the compass that steadies every decision you make.

3. Pathos—your beliefs and emotional landscape

Pathos is your emotional landscape, the beliefs, feelings, and reactions that guide or hijack your momentum. Trace what you're carrying: the expectations you've absorbed, the needs you prioritize above your own, and the stories you've internalized about worth. Emotional over-functioning can become an identity, especially for those of us who equate love with being needed. We take on what isn't ours. We overextend to be helpful, needed, indispensable. And somewhere along the way, we forget what it feels like to move from desire instead of obligation. This, too, is pathos.

4. Logos—the "stories"—both fiction and non-fiction—that you tell yourself

Logos is how you make sense of things—the stories, both fiction and fact, that shape your understanding of the world. Bring structure to your thoughts; turn vague knowing into clear articulation. This is where you begin shaping your next message, decision, or move.

It's also where the inner critic camps out, where self-doubt spins half-truths, and where SWINI offers her unsolicited commentary. But logos is your opportunity to push back—to rewrite the script, to name what's true instead of letting the noise decide for you.

5. Exigence and Kairos—two ancient Greek terms that reflect urgency and timing

This anchor helps you identify the urgency, if there is one. It helps you honor the timing. It will help you recognize that readiness is often inconvenient, but always instructive. This tool doesn't just show you where you are. It reflects why you've arrived here and what you might finally be ready to choose next.

You Don't Have to Know. You Just Have to Notice

In the coming pages, I'll walk you through each of the five anchors—not as a how-to, but as a series of reflections to help you tune your Leadership Compass. You'll learn what each anchor reflects, why it matters, and how you can use simple prompts to look at yourself honestly and move forward with clarity.

Remember, it is a *return*, not a *race*.

The Leadership Compass is something you *listen to*. There's a quiet power in hearing yourself admit: "I don't know what's next, but I know this isn't it." That's the moment sovereign leadership begins. Not with confidence, but with honesty. The Leadership Compass doesn't tell you where to go. It tells you what you already know. And it's from that inner knowing that everything else unfolds.

PART 2

The Leadership Compass in Motion

Seeing the stories is only the beginning. The real work begins when you start living differently inside them; when you stop performing, start paying attention, and learn to move from alignment instead of approval. This is where the Leadership Compass takes shape. In the pages ahead, you'll learn to read your surroundings, your emotions, and yourself with new eyes. You'll begin to sense when the moment calls for stillness, when it calls for courage, and when it calls for something in between.

This next section is where the Leadership Compass starts to make sense on the page. If you don't have it yet, you can download it at lizholtzinger.com.

CHAPTER 4

Reading the Room

What Context Explains When Clarity Can't

Before we can lead others, we have to know where we're standing. This chapter centers on one of the Leadership Compass's clearest guide points: context—the room you're in. And "room" doesn't just mean four walls. It's the city you live in. The institution you work for. The generation you were shaped by. It's the silent expectations, the unspoken codes, the emotional temperature. Context reveals what's possible—and what's quietly denied.

What Room Are You In?

Before you blame yourself for not showing up differently, ask yourself: "What room am I in?"

I've been in plenty of rooms, especially large-group meetings, where I felt off. I wasn't intimidated, exactly. Just uncertain. There were lots of people I perceived as being "more" than me. More experienced, more connected, more essential. I wasn't sure what I was doing there, what role I was meant to play. I didn't feel small, but I didn't feel seen.

But in smaller rooms? I shine. Even if someone has more experience or clout, I can "get it" faster and feel out where my voice fits.

It's not about whether you can swim (fun fact—I can't!). It's about whether the water was ever meant to hold your kind of movement. Some rooms are made for your flow. Others fight it at every turn.

Context doesn't just influence you. It reveals you.

When Clarity Fails to Land

Many leadership frameworks begin with internal clarity. And yes, clarity matters. That's what the Leadership Compass helps surface: what's true for you, what you value, what you see clearly now.

But clarity doesn't float freely. It needs a container to land in. And that container—your context—determines whether clarity resonates or gets dismissed, distorted, or ignored.

I remember sitting in a university committee meeting knowing exactly what I wanted to say. And I stayed silent. I could feel the resistance in the room, the silent hierarchy that said, "You're not on the tenure track. This isn't your lane."

The reality of a non-tenure line teaching professor who is the "Head of Household" is that some sort of supplemental income is required. So later in my career I did some work in healthcare. While working in that field, I found the same mismatch. At first, I blamed myself: for not being smarter, for not communicating better, for not knowing more.

But clarity wasn't the issue. I was speaking the language of human psychology—of persuasion, motivation, meaning. But the room was wired for status quo: keep things stable, keep things moving, don't rock the boat. Dysfunction was tolerated, even when the metrics weren't met. *Especially* when the metrics weren't met.

It wasn't that I wasn't clear. It was that the context couldn't metabolize what I was offering.

Once again, I expected myself to swim upstream—without a map, a lifeguard, or even someone to ask, "Are you okay out here?"

And yes, if this sounds familiar, it should: It's not about whether you can swim (still can't!). It's about whether the water was ever meant to hold your kind of movement.

Clarity is essential. But it's not everything. You have to know which rooms let you move with steady presence and which ones punish you for not making a splash.

Context Isn't Just a Setting—It's a Situation

We often treat context as scenery—background noise that surrounds the real action. But in leadership, communication, and everyday decision-making, context *is* the situation. It doesn't just frame the moment. It defines what's possible inside it.

Some communication theorists have tried to name this.

Among them, Lloyd Bitzer argued that every rhetorical moment emerges from an external situation: There's a problem, an audience, and a set of constraints.[1] In his view, we respond to the demands of the moment; we don't invent them.

Richard Vatz, however, pushed back.[2] He believed we don't just respond to situations; we create them by naming them. It's not the moment that defines the meaning. It's the meaning we assign to the moment. Framing *is* power.

Both are true. And both matter for sovereign leadership. Sometimes, the moment demands a response. Other times, you step in and reframe the moment entirely.

I once did that early in my academic career. I was a young lecturer, newly hired, sitting in a room full of instructors led by the director of the writing program. We were being asked to teach an assignment called Lifeboat Ethics—a hypothetical scenario where students would rank who deserves to survive a Titanic-like disaster.

The assignment, according to the director, was meant as a "thinking exercise"—a way to help students practice making tough decisions and generating clear criteria to support their recommendations. It aligned with the rhetorical goals of the recommendation essay we were all scheduled to teach, but the timing made it impossible to ignore the deeper harm.

It was just a few months after 9/11, and several of my students were from New York City. They were still raw.

Shaken. Some had family members directly impacted by the attacks.

Asking them to simulate the act of deciding who lives and who dies? That wasn't just provocative. It was insensitive. Contextually deaf. Unnecessary.

I said as much—in front of the director and my colleagues. I didn't just push back in private. I named what felt out of step. I questioned the ethics of the lesson, not just its timing.

And in my own classroom, I didn't teach Lifeboat Ethics the way I was instructed. I reframed the assignment entirely. I brought it to my students as a case study in pedagogical design. I asked them: "What do you think of this assignment? Who benefits from it? Who might it harm? What else could we do instead?"

I turned the lesson into a conversation about context. And in doing so, I challenged an unspoken rule:

Don't challenge the container.

Don't question the curriculum.

Don't make the invisible power structure visible.

I'd responded to the situation (Bitzer).

I'd named and reframed it (Vatz).

And the result?

I stepped on an institutional landmine.

Not all at once—but over time.

I would not allow my students to get hurt.

But I certainly took the bullet for them.

There were closed-door meetings; performance reviews that stung more than they guided (remember the letter and "Clara" from the book's opening anecdote?); corrections that felt less like mentorship and more like a warning: "You are not bending the knee."

I'll never know the full impact of that choice, but I felt its ripple for years—right up until the director retired. It wasn't dramatic, just a quiet door closing on a chapter that had shaped me more than I'd realized. Every leader brings joy to a group—some when they arrive, and some when they leave. On the day of her retirement, I was one of many who raised a glass to toast her departure.

Sometimes, telling the truth doesn't shift the system. It just clarifies the room you're in and the power structures that are too rigid to hold dissent.

That's context.

It doesn't just influence what you say. It shapes whether you'll be heard and what it might cost you.

How Sovereign Leaders Work with Context

Sovereign leaders don't just name the room. They learn to read *what kind* of room they're in.

Context lives on three layers: systemic, situational, and self. Each holds power. Each shapes how your clarity lands.

Systemic context is the slow-shaping layer. It's the town in which you were born; in which you were raised; in which you live. It's the culture you were trained in. It's the institution you work for. It's the generation you were born into. You don't choose systemic contexts, but they shape how you understand power, voice, authority, and safety.

Psychologist and researcher Jean Twenge, in her book *Generations*, explores how defining events—wars, recessions, technologies, cultural upheavals—shape each generation's worldview and behavior.[3] I saw this play out firsthand. I came of age as a Gen X female in institutions still shaped by the Silent Generation. In undergrad, an English major, I challenged the idea that authorial intent was absolute. I believed reader interpretation mattered.

But my professors—stoic, Silent Generation males—shut that down. They weren't being cruel. They just couldn't see through my lens. Their world had taught them to privilege the author. Mine had started to ask, "What about the reader?"

In the context of these professors, I was asking the wrong questions and giving the wrong answers.

But I wasn't wrong. Those Silent Generation males weren't wrong, either. We just wore different glasses.

Situational context is what's happening right now. It's the dynamic in the room—the power structure, emotional temperature, unspoken rules. Are people calm or defensive? Open or guarded? It's the atmosphere, right now.

Ignoring this layer risks bulldozing truth into people who aren't ready to hold it.

I'm reminded of Ava Daniels in season 1 of Max's *Hacks*, the 25-year-old Gen Z writer whose clarity often collides with the context around her. It's not that she's wrong. It's that she doesn't yet see how tone, timing, and power ("the room") shape what's heard. Her conversations with Boomer comedian Deborah Vance are filled with subtle missteps: speaking too fast, too bluntly, too soon. She hasn't learned to read the room—not just for mood, but for hierarchy.

That was my younger self, too: determined to speak what felt true; eager to name what felt off. While I'd read the assignment, I didn't read the room. Especially not when that room included the director of the writing program. I didn't see that clarity, in some contexts, gets read as disrespect. And I didn't understand yet that respect was something the room's leader expected *before* they would offer it in return.

I misread what the moment could metabolize.

Neither truth nor clarity guarantee safety.

Context determines whether your truth lands—with authority—or fractures the room, maybe even your career.

Self-context is your internal weather. Are you clear or cloudy? Centered or reactive? Calm or scattered? Your body holds context, too. If your nervous system is in overdrive, it doesn't matter how solid your strategy is—it won't land. If you're exhausted, you might misread neutrality as rejection. If you're hyper-focused, you might miss the signal that says, "Now isn't the moment."

When I feel grounded, I know exactly how to lead. I listen better. I interpret resistance more accurately. I don't make everything personal.

Sometimes I feel...blank. Bored. Unmoved. And I catch myself wondering if something's wrong. If I'm missing the signal. If I've lost momentum. But maybe boredom isn't always a problem. Maybe it's just what clarity feels like—when nothing urgent is pulling at you. When you're not reacting. When you're just...present.

Self-context doesn't mean fixing yourself. It means noticing your state before you try to lead anyone else.

What to Listen For

Once you learn to name the kinds of context you're in, you start to hear things differently. Not every silence means agreement; not every nod means understanding; not every "yes" means readiness.

Knowing your truth is one thing. Knowing when and how it can land—that's something else entirely. That's when you start listening for the room. That means asking:

- What's being tolerated here but not supported?
- Who has power, and what do they need in order to feel safe enough to hear truth?
- Is this the moment to say it—or just to *see* it?

If I could go back to that faculty meeting again; if I could talk to my younger self, I wouldn't silence her entirely. I'd just whisper: "Read the room. Respect doesn't always flow freely. In some rooms, it's transactional. Conditional. Hierarchical. If you must absolutely get this off your chest, speak with the director privately. And even still, Liz, proceed with caution."

What I didn't know then—but know now—is that some people expect deference before they offer respect. And if you question them *without first praising them*, you won't be seen as bold. You'll be seen as disloyal.

That moment—where clarity met a wall of hierarchy—stayed with me. It taught me something I couldn't have learned from books alone: Some rooms have rules that aren't spoken; some power structures require performance before permission; and some truths can only be delivered when the container is strong enough to hold them.

So now, I listen. For what's *not* said. For how tone shifts in the presence of a leader. For whether someone's clarity can actually land there.

Sovereign leaders don't just read the room; they listen for its limits.

The Invitation to Reframe

I've always believed in the value of having a mentor, guide, or coach, someone who can see the bigger picture when you're too close to your own details. A good coach doesn't tell you what to do; they help you see what's already there. They hold perspective when yours narrows. Sometimes that perspective is affirming, and sometimes it's uncomfortable—but it's always instructive.

Even so, perspective can be tested, especially when the very person meant to offer it misses the moment.

When a moment feels off—tense, stuck, or imbalanced—it's easy to blame the people in the room. It's also easy to blame yourself. Or to assume the worst about what just happened.

But sovereign leaders don't stop at frustration. They zoom out. They ask:

- What's shaping this moment?
- Was the commitment clear?
- Was the context aligned?
- Was I expecting something this setup couldn't actually hold?

I found myself asking those very questions after my business coach missed a call—twice. A call they had scheduled. A call I was paying for. Their absence felt careless. Disrespectful. And I was ready to make it mean something about them.

But then I paused.

What if it wasn't personal?

What if this wasn't about them at all—but maybe a weak structure? A wobbly setup? A jammed schedule? A typo in the calendar, perhaps? A container that couldn't hold what I needed?

That's the invitation: Before blaming the people in the room, step back and look at what's holding the moment together or letting it fall apart.

Not all missed moments are betrayals. Some are structural. Some are misaligned. Some are simply too small for what you're trying to carry or for what you need.

Sovereign leaders don't shrink themselves to fit a faulty frame. They build better containers or step outside them entirely, and eventually, I stepped out of that one.

Seeing the Room, Seeing Yourself

You don't always need to take big action. Sometimes, the first move is just learning to read the room. That's what context helps you do.

- You can look outward:
  Are the expectations clear? Are the roles defined? Is the moment structured or slipping?

- You can look at the moment:
  Do I feel safe here? Trusted? Or am I bracing, performing, self-editing?

- And you can look inward:
  Am I grounded enough to respond? Or am I reaching for resolution too quickly?

These are context cues. They don't always shout. Sometimes they whisper.

You don't have to decode every dynamic, but you *do* need to notice how the room is shaping you. Because once you name the room—you get to choose what to do with it: Stay. Shift it. Or step out.

What's Next?

You can't control every room, but you can learn how to read one. The more clearly you see the room, the more clearly you can see yourself in it.

Context doesn't always change what you say, but it often changes *how* and *when* you say it. And sometimes, it changes whether you say it at all.

In the next chapter, we'll move from reading the room to owning your voice within it. We'll talk about ethos—not as an academic term, but as a personal one. Ethos is about your trustworthiness and credibility.

Spoiler Alert: Ethos doesn't come from your job title or any of the "roles" you play.

It comes from your consistency; from how you carry your clarity; from who you become—over time, in practice, in motion.

CHAPTER 5

Who Are You Without the Title?

You Don't Earn Credibility. You Return to It

Iused to think I knew who I was. Wife. Teacher. Aunt. Cousin. Daughter. Professor.

But when my husband, Jeff, died in October 2013, one of those roles—the one I'd worn longest and tried hardest to hold onto—disappeared. And with it, something unspoken collapsed: the scaffolding I'd built my identity around.

No one tells you how disorienting it is to lose a title before you're ready to give it up. I wasn't just grieving a complicated marriage. I was grieving the version of myself who knew where she stood in a room because of who she stood next to.

That's when the question began to surface: "If I'm not a wife anymore...who am I?"

The grief was suffocating—terrifying, even. I had never felt so low. The truth that haunted me most was this: He hadn't treated me kindly when he was alive. He was oil, and I was water, and if a match was ever lit near him, he turned into an unholy hellfire. His abuse burned hot and wide, scorching anyone too close, including me. Mostly me. My water could never douse it. When he died, that fire finally went out, but it left me standing in the smoke, unsure of who I was without it.

In the quiet, I begged God to take me. I didn't want there to be a tomorrow. I was that hollow. That lost. Night after night, I prayed the same prayer—simple, desperate, unchanging. I asked for release, for rest, for the ache to end. And when the sun rose anyway, I took it as both mercy and punishment. Each morning felt like proof that God wasn't finished with me yet—even if I wished He were.

But something shifted—slowly, and then all at once. Maybe it was the holidays creeping in just weeks after. Maybe it was the weight of seeing everyone else wrapped in joy while I felt like I was still crawling through ash. Whatever it was, something inside me cracked open and spoke with a clarity I had not heard from myself for a really long time: "Fuck this. This sucks. And I don't want to live this way."

I didn't mourn for long. I cut my losses—literally—and moved on. I didn't want to just *survive* my life anymore. I wanted to *live* it. Really live it. To enjoy it. To find someone who wanted to enjoy it with me rather than steal all the joy out of life.

And that moment—*that decision*—was the beginning of something different. Not a reinvention. A return.

Why This Matters to You: What Ethos Solves

Loss takes many forms. Maybe you've changed jobs, left a relationship, or simply woken up one morning and realized you no longer recognize yourself. However it arrives, the question is the same: "Who am I now?"

Harris III—an author and storyteller whose work on identity and imagination has shaped countless conversations in leadership and personal growth—writes in his book, *The Wonder Switch*, about inciting incidents—those disorienting, sometimes painful moments that interrupt the narrative we've been living.[1] Suddenly, the story no longer fits. And we're left standing in the middle of a life that demands a new script.

I think of Jean Valjean in Victor Hugo's *Les Misérables*—a man whose life is marked by one inciting moment after another. Released from prison. Rejected by the world. Shown mercy by a bishop. Each moment forces a deeper reckoning: *Who am I now?* What do I owe others? What do I owe myself?

Valjean's journey isn't about reclaiming a reputation. It's about reorienting to a different kind of credibility—the kind that isn't given by the world, but chosen from within.

That's ethos.

Ethos isn't something you inherit. It's something you practice. It's not a brand. It's not a performance. It's the core of who you are and how you choose to move through the world—especially after everything familiar has fallen away.

Ethos isn't about building confidence. Ethos is about returning to coherence. When the script gets ripped from your hands, your *character* becomes another anchor.

Ethos, Misunderstood

In a world obsessed with branding, ethos reminds us: Credibility isn't curated. It's revealed.

Previously, when I introduced the Leadership Compass, I mentioned that its roots weren't just metaphorical. They were rhetorical. As in: Aristotle rhetorical. Aristotle believed that every act of persuasion—every attempt to lead, influence, or connect—relies on three appeals: ethos (credibility), pathos (emotion), and logos (logic). These weren't just philosophical terms. They were deeply human ways of understanding how we build trust and create meaning.

He broke ethos down into three traits:

- *Phrónēsis* (froh-nay-sis)—practical wisdom

- *Aretē* (ah-reh-tay)—moral character

- *Eunoia* (yoo-noy-uh)—goodwill toward the audience

Try casually dropping "eunoia" into a dinner conversation and watch people slowly back away. (Ask me how I know.) These terms might sound like something you'd scrawl in the margins of a philosophy textbook to help you study for a test—and yes, I did (and I still failed the test; I was never a good "test taker").

Ethos isn't about résumé bullets. It's about resonance; it's your character, in motion. We often mistake polish for presence. We over-index on optics. But people don't trust polish. They trust *alignment.* Truth.

In academia, credibility is sometimes measured by degrees and publications. In gyms, it's about aesthetics and numbers on a barbell. In corporate offices, it's about job titles, revenue and profits, and LinkedIn headlines. In parenting groups, it's who has the best routine or calmest toddler. In every sphere, there's a metric. But none of those prove *character.*

I've experienced several of these systems—the assumptions, the projections, the dismissals. I've taught my students that writers and speakers can demonstrate credibility through citing appropriate sources and maintaining proper grammar, tone, and organization—and yes, that matters. But let's be honest: In person, we often *just know* when someone is trustworthy. There's an energy. A resonance. An ethos. With writing and speaking, we sometimes have to overcompensate to make it obvious: "Look how credible I am!"

Ethos doesn't beg to be believed. It just is.

The Role of Rupture in Revealing Character

Rupture doesn't give you ethos. It reveals what was already there.

After Jeff died, I didn't just lose a husband. I lost the scaffolding I had built my sense of identity upon. And while the grief was thick and contradictory, there was space underneath all that weight. Space I hadn't had before. Space that invited me back to myself.

Yes, I clung to the old story. I even rewrote parts of it to protect his memory and protect myself because I was embarrassed by how bad things had sometimes gotten. But I also kept showing up—for myself. Much to the shock of my colleagues, I went back to work shortly after his death. I kept working out (I was competitive in physique shows back in those days), and I started saying yes to yoga again.

Years earlier, I used to wake up at 6 a.m. and follow Steve Ross's yoga program *Inhale* on the Oxygen Channel. I'd roll out my $6 Walmart mat, ease into downward dog to the groovy tunes of the '70s, and let this nontraditional, joy-filled yoga guide help me start my day. Jeff used to mock me for it. Thought it was a joke. And more than once, he suggested I stop taking the class because it woke *him* up too early—because my joy, my routine, my small slice of morning peace was inconvenient to his sleep.

But I loved yoga.

And post-rupture, yoga became a small act of rebellion and restoration. I returned to it not to escape—but to feel more like myself.

Through it all, something emerged—something already waiting: a woman who was not broken but buried.

While rupture often forces that emergence, not everyone needs a rupture to experience clarity. An inciting incident? Yes. But it doesn't have to be trauma or tragedy. Sometimes the wake-up call is quiet. Sometimes it's a lyric. A conversation. A reunion. A meeting. A Broadway show. A yoga class.

Kerry as Mirror, Not Savior

Ethos came alive for me in a restorative yoga class at PYP Studio. My dear friend Amy brought me. She knew what I needed in those early days after Jeff's passing, even when I didn't. I was exhausted. Grief-stricken. Barely eating. She brought me food—weeks' worth of meals—and then gently invited me to a restorative yoga class. I arrived raw and guarded.

The class ended in savasana, a resting pose often offered at the end of yoga. I was scared. This was unfamiliar territory, and I wasn't sure how I'd be received—or if I even belonged. But as I lay there, Kerry Bestwick—the studio's owner and leader of the class—walked over, knelt above my head, gently held me, and touched my brow.[2] She said: "You are whole. You are complete. Just as you are."

In that moment, an enormous weight lifted off my shoulders. I not only felt like I belonged—I felt accepted. As I was. And with what I was carrying. It was, without a doubt, what Harris III would call an inciting moment. It changed me.

I broke. I cried. I unclenched. Something softened in me that hadn't softened in years. Kerry didn't save me. She *mirrored* me. And that reflection—brief as it was—changed everything.

Choosing Who to Be: From Expectation Boulevard to ABC

Kerry would later become more than a yoga teacher to me. She was, at that point, already a coach, a speaker, and a facilitator of leadership development programs. She had a way of bridging wellness, mindset, and identity.

I first encountered the Be–Do–Have model through Kerry's 40-day program—a guided journey that combined journaling, meditation, nutrition, and reflection to help participants shift from autopilot living to intentional being. It asked us not what we wanted to have, but who we wanted to become.

The ideas stirred something in me, something I couldn't shake. It was the first time I truly understood that identity could lead action, not just follow it.

Before I knew about Be–Do–Have, I lived on what I called Expectation Boulevard. You know the road: Go to college. Pick a practical major. Graduate in four years. Get married. Have kids. Stay put. Stay good.

I didn't resent the structure. The traditional path—marriage, family, domestic life—seemed like a reasonable way to live. But I was misaligned—both in who I was at the time and in who I partnered with. That life couldn't flourish under those conditions. The expectations I tried to live up to didn't match the reality I was living. So when Kerry introduced the Be–Do–Have model, everything cracked open.

Most of us live backwards: Once I *have* the job, the partner, the title, then I can *do* the things that make me feel confident. And finally, I'll *be* the person I want to be.

But real transformation begins with identity. BE first. Then DO. Then HAVE.

I believed in this model so deeply that I invited Kerry to co-present with me to my students one semester. We gathered them in a campus theater one evening—not for extra credit, but for transformation. That night was electric. We taught. We laughed. We asked big questions:

- Who do you want to BE?

- How do you want to move through the world?

- What happens when you lead from that place?

At first, the BE I chose was "awake and aware." It was a beginning—a way to move from Old Story Liz to Better Story Liz. Nearly a decade later, when I co-launched AguaVivir, a wellness-focused IV infusion start-up, I began navigating the complexities of sales and marketing in healthcare when I came across Dan Pink's book *To Sell Is Human*—a book about sales that, unexpectedly, gave language to something deeper [3].

In it, he redefines ABC—not as Always Be Closing—but as:

- *Attunement*—the ability to read others and remain present

- *Buoyancy*—the resilience to stay afloat in rejection

- *Clarity*—the capacity to communicate what's essential

These weren't just good sales traits. They were good *human* traits. They resonated deeply, so I reframed them for myself:

- *Attuned*—present, perceptive, responsive
- *Buoyant*—emotionally light, able to rise
- *Clear*—honest, transparent, rooted in truth

Those became my ethos—not a brand, not a costume, but a *way of being*. Not just in the workplace. Not just in the classroom. *In life.*

Years later, in 2024, I sat in a Broadway theater watching *The Great Gatsby* come alive on stage. As a sucker for a good book and an even bigger sucker for musicals, I was already enchanted. But this time, something else clicked: Every character in that story lives the Be–Do–Have model in reverse. Gatsby believed that if he could *have* Daisy, he could *do* what it took to win her love and finally *be* fulfilled.

Daisy wanted to *have* security, so she could *do* what was expected and *be* content.

Nick sought to *have* adventure, hoping it would help him *do* something meaningful, so he could *be* significant. Tom simply wanted to *have it all*, assuming that would let him *do* whatever he pleased and *be* invincible.

And none of them got what they wanted. Because they never started with the most important question: Who do I want to BE? That question still guides me. And the answer changes everything.

Ethos in Sovereign Leadership

People won't follow your credentials. They'll follow your coherence.

Sovereign leadership—how you lead yourself—isn't about role or rank. It's not about your job title or your résumé. It's about presence. Integrity. Wholeness.

When you lead from ethos, people feel your credibility. You become a mirror for their own courage. Your clarity gives others permission to be honest. Your steadiness becomes the safety they didn't know they needed.

Here's the key: Ethos isn't a role. It's a rhythm. It's not about being a CEO, a teacher, a coach, or even a parent. It's about how you move through your world—your context— with consistency, integrity, and care. It's your tone. Your stance. Your default setting when things get uncertain.

I've seen what happens when people lead from a role. The trying-too-hard. The defensiveness. The disconnection. And I've also seen what's possible when someone leads from ethos. It's unforgettable.

So, if you're wondering where to start? Start here:

- Who do you want to BE—not just at work, but in life?

- What three qualities do you want people to *feel* when they're around you?

- What would change if you lived those qualities on purpose?

You don't need a new title. You don't need a massive rebrand. You just need a shift in center.

Ethos isn't about being liked. It's about being trusted. And trust is earned through alignment.

The Character That Carries You

Roles change. Titles expire. Credentials fade. But the character you build from? That stays.

You don't need to become someone new. It's about remembering who you've always been—beneath the job description, the expectations, the degrees, the storylines you've outgrown.

Ethos is not something you earn. It's something you embody, and the moment you choose to BE—on purpose, with clarity—you begin leading yourself home.

So if you're in the middle of your own shift, here's what I want you to know:

You don't need to wait for the next title to lead.

You don't need a platform to make an impact.

You don't need to have it all figured out to be trustworthy.

What you need is a starting point. A question.

Ask yourself this: "Who do I want to BE, no matter what happens next?"

Then move from there.

Next up: We'll talk about how to work with the emotions, beliefs, and attachments that shape what we do and why: pathos. Because if ethos is your center, pathos is what moves you forward or keeps you stuck.

CHAPTER 6

What Moves You
(And What Shouldn't)

Emotions Bubble Up.
It's Your Job to Tell Them What to Do

You've already met ethos (credibility, character) and explored how your context shapes your leadership. Now, it's pathos's turn. Pathos isn't easy to write about. Probably because it's the part of the Leadership Compass I've wrestled with the most.

I've made a lot of decisions in my life that might have looked "right" on the surface: stayed when it seemed to be the kind thing to do; gave when I had nothing left; showed up, followed through, kept the peace. I told myself I was leading from values—loyalty, service, love. But the truth? I was leading from unchecked emotion—mistaking reactivity for compassion, and exhaustion for love.

Pathos, Misunderstood

The Leadership Compass is a model for leading yourself with alignment. Pathos is its emotional anchor point. It's not about being emotional or emotionless. It's about *knowing what your emotions are asking of you.*

Aristotle said pathos was one of the three pillars of persuasion—alongside ethos and logos—and he tied it directly to values. Pathos connects to what we care about, to the emotions that rise when our values are honored—or violated. But he never meant for pathos to be in charge.

In modern life, pathos has been flattened. Think of political ads that try to scare or shock you into voting one way. Or the "sad puppy" charity spots that pull tears but rarely offer a clear plan for action for resolving foundational problems. The ASPCA's commercials from a few years back—set to Sarah McLachlan's "Angel"—were a masterclass in pure pathos. I was a complete sucker. I donated. And then I couldn't even walk past the TV when they aired, because it made me so sad.

Juxtapose that with the UNICEF commercials featuring Alyssa Milano. Those didn't move me at all. I know, I know... what does it say that I gave to help animals but not people? (I'm still not sure.) But that's the nature of overindulged pathos. It pulls hard, but not always evenly, and not always toward action that's balanced with reason.

What we miss is this: Emotions are just messengers. They arrive on the scene before the story is fully written.

You don't need to silence them. You need to translate them. To clarify...

Not all fear means stop.

Not all guilt means you owe.

Not all hope means it's worth waiting for.

Sometimes those feelings are relics. Echoes. Outdated stories bubbling up in present-day clothing.

If ethos is who you are, then pathos is what you feel—and logos, which we'll explore in the next chapter, is how you make sense of it all. For now, know this: All three work together. None can carry the load alone.

I learned that the hard way. For years, I let pathos lead unchecked—convinced I was acting from values when I was really just obeying my emotions. That confusion came to a head in one of the most pivotal and painful seasons of my life.

When Fear Wears a Halo

In 2003, I married my first husband, Jeff. By September of that year, I discovered he was cheating. (And yes, this is the same guy I was talking about in a previous chapter.)

I'd been watching TV in the basement and made my way upstairs to go to bed when I heard him quietly talking on the phone. His tone was soft—softer than I'd ever heard it. I paused and listened. And I knew.

We had just gotten married that May. To go from "newlywed" to "betrayed" in just a few months was emotional whiplash of the highest order—disorienting, destabilizing, and devastating.

He denied it, of course—for days. But the evidence kept surfacing. And eventually, I left. Walked out on the marriage. Said we should separate.

But then? I came back. I told myself I was a Christian and that God would be upset with me if I divorced. I stayed out of some idealized notion of "virtue." On the surface, it looked like I was holding to my values. It looked like I was returning because I felt love.

But what I really felt—and shared with no one—felt nothing like love. It was fear: fear I'd lose everything; fear I'd have to pay him alimony because on paper, I made more money than he did. I was so afraid of losing money I couldn't afford to lose that I didn't even meet with an attorney because I feared the cost of a first consultation and any additional meetings that would be a part of the process. And I feared what it would mean for a Holtzinger to divorce. The shame was heavy before I'd even said the word out loud.

Beneath all of that lived another fear I never said out loud: the fear that even if I left, he wouldn't. That ending the marriage wouldn't end the hold. That he would stay attached, present, woven into my life in ways I couldn't untangle. It wasn't love. It was the sense that his need for me — or for what I provided — would continue no matter what I chose. And I didn't yet trust myself to stand up to that kind of pull.

To add insult to injury, I found out the affair had started much earlier than he admitted, long before we were married—and that it continued to grow even after I found out, though he vehemently denied it. I kept sinking inside myself, questioning over and over: "Could this really be happening? Maybe I'm making it all up. Maybe these stories in my head are just that—stories."

For the next ten years, pathos stayed in charge—fear, shame, and doubt dictating my choices.

The cost? Rage.

Not just frustration or bitterness. I carried a soul-deep rage that roared through my body like static. Rage I couldn't name, couldn't speak, couldn't act on; the kind of rage that makes you wish the adulterer himself were dead.

I found a strange comfort in heavy metal music at the time—Rage Against the Machine, Korn, Slipknot. These bands were on my iPod, the theme music for every workout. They blared in my ears as I tried to move the weight of my own silence. That music helped me channel what I couldn't say out loud, what I couldn't scream in real life. It was a form of emotional regulation before I had language for that term. A way to survive when nothing else felt safe.

That rage lived in me for years, simmering under the surface, until...one day, my "wish came true" in 2013 when he actually *did* die... With his death came a different weight altogether. The fear that had ruled me for years was gone, but it was replaced by guilt. A low-grade, persistent, soul-humming grief laced with survivor's guilt.

That's what happens when you let emotion—in this case, fear, and later, guilt—rule without question. You think you're doing the right thing because you've managed to connect your staying with your so-called "core values." Um. Hello,

Halo? You think you're "paying your penance" by being the "sad widow," and I *was* sad. For a time. Until I realized I was now being abusive to myself, abandoning myself and erasing myself, over and over. By the time I could see it clearly, the damage had been done, and the patterns were ingrained.

But *recognition* is where the shift starts.

Once I named what had been happening—that fear, guilt, and shame had been steering my decisions for more than a decade—I could start asking different questions. I could practice making space between the feeling and the action.

There have been plenty of times since then when pathos has tried to take the wheel—and just as many times when I've managed to keep my hands on it. One of the clearest examples happened in more recent history, when it didn't arrive as betrayal or grief, but as physical symptoms I couldn't explain. No big story. No obvious villain. Just a body in alarm mode.

And this time, I didn't hand over the keys.

When the Body Sends Weird "Feeling" Signals

Heart flutters. Sleepless nights. Fatigue. Major GI distress. A tight, unshakable panic with no obvious source. There was no big event. No heartbreak. No villain. Just a body in alarm mode—for *months*.

I went to doctors. Ran bloodwork and tests—EKGs, ultrasounds, the works! Everything came back normal.

In the past, those physical symptoms would have been all the invitation pathos needed to take over. I would have filled in the blanks with fear and let the worst-case scenarios dictate my choices.

This time, I used something my therapist had taught me years earlier: the "And Then What Happens" game. It's simple, but it's relentless. You name what you're afraid of, and then ask yourself, "And then what happens?" over and over until you've chased the story all the way to its end.

For me, it went something like this: *These heart palpitations mean something is wrong with my heart.*

And then what happens? *There's something medically wrong with me, and it's going to require that someone take care of me.*

And then what happens? *G* (my current life partner who is *beyond* amazing) *leaves me because I've become a burden.*

And then what happens? *I won't be able to take care of myself.*

And then what happens? *I'll die.*

And then what happens? *Nothing; it's all over.*

The real fear, then, wasn't about heart palpitations at all. It was about fearing G would leave me to fend for myself, a fear I can roll my eyes at now for its absurdity. He wouldn't do that. It's not in him to walk away and abandon someone he loves. It was also about fearing I wouldn't be able to take care of myself. But if I look at my record so far, I've 100% "made it." I'm still here—living proof that I *can* take care of myself.

Underneath that all was the deeper fear: dying and not being okay with dying. And yet, death is something none of us can escape—making that fear, too, irrational.

But my therapist never let me stop there. Once we'd chased the fear to its end, she'd have me run the story again, this time looking for another possible version and putting me in the driver's seat.

So let's start over: *These heart palpitations mean something is wrong with my heart.*

And then what happens? *I go to the doctor, and they find the problem early.*

And then what happens? *I get treatment, and it works.*

And then what happens? *I recover. I live.*

Two completely different endings. Same starting point.

That's the space where self-leadership happens. I didn't ignore what my body was telling me. I stayed attuned (remember ethos?). I checked in with logos—getting the tests, gathering the data. And I let pathos *inform* my perspective, but didn't allow it to *make* my decisions for me.

Choosing from the Center

When emotions rise now, I take a lesson from an old fire drill.

Stop. Drop. Roll.

I *stop* and assess what's actually happening. Not what I *feel* is happening—but what's true.

I *drop* the old stories that used to rush in and latch onto every sensation.

And I let the feeling *roll* off—or at least, I do something to help it move—unless the pause reveals that there really is an emergency.

That's the key difference now. I don't assume every strong emotion is a signal to act. I treat it like a check engine light. Pause. Assess. Don't panic.

And in that pause, I remind myself: "I am not this feeling. And this feeling is not me." It's just a spark. It's not the fire.

Sometimes I take myself through a logical progression of questions.

- Is this emotion valid?
- Is the story I'm connecting to it one I actually believe or just one I've inherited?
- Does this align with who I want to be?

Even now, I sometimes lose to pathos—far less than before, and I recognize it faster when it happens. But still...I sometimes lose. I am, after all, human.

The mistake isn't feeling pathos. The mistake is believing it *should* lead and allowing it to lead *all of the time.*

Empathy is beautiful. But it's not always a green light.

Sometimes I feel deep compassion for someone, but that doesn't mean I'm required to act on it.

Sometimes I feel compassion for myself, but that doesn't mean I give in to every emotional pull.

I have to ask:

Does this action align with my ethos—am I BEING attuned, buoyant, clear?

Does this fit within the context I'm currently living in?

Does this support my priorities?

If it doesn't, I let it pass.

Because leadership—real leadership—starts at the center. It's not a mood. It's a muscle. It's the spine that holds your yes and your no.

And when I choose from that place?

My body knows. My torso feels stable. My breath is steady. My legs say, "We've got you."

Integration Is the Goal

Context. Ethos. Pathos.

By now, you've seen each of these points of the Leadership Compass on their own. But none of them work in isolation. There is no first step, second step, third. There's an understanding of each part and then an integration of all three into your daily life.

When you lead from *only* pathos, you might look compassionate or loyal. But if it's unchecked, it can lead you straight into burnout, resentment, and decisions rooted in fear or guilt. I know this because I've been there. I've lived the cost—an unfulfilling marriage, a draining career, and a version of myself I barely recognized.

Cut pathos out completely, and you get a different problem: You lose connection. You can become strategic and "effective" on paper, but cold and disconnected in reality. You risk alienating the very people—and parts of yourself—that you're supposed to lead.

Sovereignty requires balance. It's like harmony in music. I recently saw the Alter Eagles, a cover band for the Eagles, performing live. Every member had a different style—one barely moved, another was all expression and flair. One mic was a little too hot, throwing off the blend now and then. But when they hit the harmonies? Everyone in the room felt it. Not because it was perfect, but because it resonated.

Even with some of the original Eagles gone, people still pay to hear their music being played by others. That's what integration creates: a sound, a presence, a legacy that lasts.

What Moves You, Now?

You don't choose the first feeling, but you do choose what it becomes.

For years, I let fear, guilt, and shame write the script for my life. I told myself I was acting on values, but really, I was just obeying emotions that knew how to dress themselves up as virtue.

Now, I know better. I still feel the pull of pathos. I still lose to it sometimes. But I don't hand it the wheel without question.

Instead, I pause. I listen. I translate. Stop, drop, roll.

Emotions are signals—not commands. They can inform my choices, but they no longer make them. And when I act, it's not because I've been swept up in a feeling but because what I'm about to do aligns with my ethos, fits my context, and supports my priorities. That's what self-leadership looks like. Not the absence of emotion, but the *integration* of it. Leading yourself doesn't start with certainty. It starts with curiosity. It starts with being willing to ask yourself: "What's this feeling trying to get me to be? And do I actually want to become that?" Stop. Drop. Roll.

Next up, we'll look at logos—the anchor of reason and clarity, the way we make sense of the world through the stories we tell ourselves and others. From there, we'll explore exigence and kairos, and finally, how it all comes together and becomes your Inner GPS.

CHAPTER 7

The Stories That Sound Like Truth

Logos Helps You Test Them

Jasmine—or Beyoncé, as she insisted we call her—sat in the back corner of the classroom, the farthest from me she could get, yet her presence was always the one most felt. When she wasn't there, the room was grayer, like someone had turned down the wattage in the lights.

She was bright, clear-eyed, stunning. She came *dressed* for class: stylish ensemble—not the sweatpants preferred by her classmates—full makeup, full set of nails. She *showed up*. And she had a way of sliding in comments that made the whole class crack up.

One day, Jasmine turned in an analysis paper quoting from a newspaper article. In the signal phrase she used to introduce the source to her readers, she referred to the "article" as a "story." The journalism bloodline in me, I smirked and bristled at the misuse. Without a moment's hesitation, I just corrected it in the margin, teacher hat firmly on: "Refer to the source as an 'article,' not a 'story.'"

Despite my "correction," she kept calling them "stories" in subsequent class conversations and essays. Over time, I saw the point she wasn't trying to make but was making anyway: Even "the news" is someone's arrangement of events, a version of reality.

It was the first time I noticed how quickly I defended the Language of Authority without asking if it deserved defending.

Choosing Stories

The most insidious "stories" are the ones we never agreed to believe. They just streamed in through people who wore some kind of authority badge: Parents. Pastors. Professors.

Some of mine:

- Jesus Christ is my Lord and Savior.
- Sex should be saved for marriage.
- Women are not trustworthy.
- Only author-intent matters; the reader has no "say" in the interpretation of a "text."

I kept the first two out of conviction; the last two cost me *decades*.

I believed I couldn't trust women, so I didn't let many of them close. Oddly enough, I didn't have a single, credible reason I could point to as to why I couldn't trust women. I just didn't. There was no name, no face, no experience to correspond to the story…just a story: Women are not trustworthy.

Then there was the "real life" poetry professor—brilliant, mercurial, convinced that *only* the author's intent for meaning mattered when reading poetry. I thought meaning was co-created between the text and reader. We sparred in class. In essay margins, there would be lots of red ink, indicating that the essay "lacks focus and direction!"

And here's the irony: He probably wasn't wrong. My essays at 19, 20, 21 years old probably *did* lack focus and direction. My *whole inner life* was a draft—messy, sprawling, scattered. The problem wasn't his observation. The problem was how I received it. Instead of separating his comments from the work, I let them *become* stories about *me*. Not about a paper, but about my capacity. I translated the commentary into "*I* lack focus and direction." I carried that story for decades… until finally, I didn't.

Stories don't just float around on their own. They take shape in the way we arrange them, repeat them, and give them authority. That arrangement—the structure of a story, the way it lands—is where logos lives. Logos isn't the opposite of story; it's the architecture that makes the story persuasive.

The Turn: Logos as the Anchor of Sense-Making

We can't talk about logos and not bring in Aristotle.

In Book I Chapter 2 of *Rhetoric*, Aristotle defines rhetoric as "the faculty of observing in any given case the available means of persuasion."[1] Rhetoric is the art of discovering how to argue so something lands and persuades. He divides persuasive proof into three appeals (two of which we've already examined): ethos (credibility), pathos (emotion), and logos (reason or arrangement). He also outlines the five canons—invention, arrangement, style, memory, delivery— the architecture that makes persuasion work.

Fast-forward to modern scholars, who continue to push the boundaries of what "logos" means. Some see "logos" as narrowly as just style or delivery, but others expand it to include logic, poetics, narrative, and argument across human communication.

What does that mean for leading yourself first? It means logos isn't the absence of story; it's the disciplined helping hand of story. Logos doesn't ask us to strip away emotion or voice. Instead, logos helps us shape them, so our stories land with truth, not just comfort.

I used to run by the script: "I'm unfocused, directionless, just impulse chasing impulse." After all, a well-constructed lie delivered by my mercurial professor once felt truer than my messy real life. With logos, I get to do a mental audit, much like I do with pathos. I can verify whether or not the story is true—for me. Logos keeps the story true. To—and for—you.

Not Every Story Gets to Lead

Aristotle called it logos. Michael McRay, head of the Istoria Institute, calls it narrative intelligence—the ability to recognize the stories you're living inside.[2] He warns that the most dangerous stories are the ones you don't know you're living. An unexamined story doesn't just color how you see the world; it quietly sets the edges of possibility. That's exactly where logos enters the conversation. Logos shines a light on those stories—not to erase them, but to test whether they still belong.

The genesis of some of our stories? Some of mine came from other people. Others came from my titles I've held. Wife. Daughter. Professor. These weren't just roles; they were entire operating systems. I didn't have to ask myself what I wanted or what was possible, because the role script was already written:

Here's what a good wife does.

Here's how a good daughter behaves.

Here's the way a good professor conducts herself.

And like all scripts, they can be comforting. But there's a catch: Even a "good" story can become a cage if you never hold it up to the light.

Logos is the flashlight. It's not that those roles or scripts are false; it's that they might not be the *whole truth*. A title is not an identity, and an identity is not a destiny. The story might be worth keeping, but only after you've decided it belongs to you—and not to whoever first handed you the script.

Some of the roles I carried were so deeply scripted that I needed a place to test them. For me, that place was journaling, and eventually I discovered that writing the story down doesn't mean letting it lead.

The Rabbit Hole Called "Journaling"

Journaling gets sold as a panacea for self-awareness. And I bought it—mostly because some "authority figure" (me) told me it was essential.

The trouble was, I wasn't excavating anything. I was just building a better bunker for my old stories. The pages became a rehearsal space for the worst lines I'd ever been given: *You're not enough. You're unfocused. You're too much here, not enough there.* Over and over, I set those words in ink, convinced the act of writing them was somehow moving me through them.

However...

A page is neutral.

It will hold your insight or your poison without judgment. If all you're putting down is fear dressed up as reflection, you're not creating clarity. You're fortifying the loop.

Metadiscourse—naming the "browser tabs" in your mind— can help break that cycle. Metadiscourse is the practice of noticing *how* you're talking to yourself, not just *what* you're saying. Logos steps in here, too: It asks if the way you've arranged your thoughts is bringing you closer to truth or just keeping you company in the lie.

When noticing wasn't enough, I found another move: I changed the audience. When I wrote only to myself, the page became an echo chamber for fear. When I started writing to God, the entries became prayers, and the loop broke. Later, when I began writing with others in mind—

not to confess, but to share what might help—the words stopped reinforcing my story and started reframing it.

Practical Logos—The Story Audit

Changing the audience helped me shift the story, but logos doesn't stop there. It also gives us tools for testing which versions to keep, which to rewrite, and which to finally release.

Here's the difference between vague self-help and actual rhetorical discipline: You don't just "notice" your stories; you interrogate them.

The Story Audit is one way to do it:

1. *Name the source.* Track the thread back to its first telling. Was it a parent? A teacher? A culture that benefits from you believing it?

2. *Test the alignment.* Does this story still fit the person you've become? Or is it stitched for a version of you that doesn't exist anymore?

3. *Rewrite or release.* If it's not true, what's truer? If it's unfixable, why carry it?

Here's what it looks like in practice. Take the story I carried for years: "Women aren't trustworthy."

Name the source: I first heard the "Women aren't trustworthy" story through my mother, who was merely retelling my grandmother's confession. Grandma Heikes had admitted she didn't trust women. But here's the thing:

I don't actually know why. Did Gramma carry that story from someone else? Or did she live through moments when women she called "friends" betrayed her? I'll never know for sure. She died before I ever had a chance to ask her.

Test the alignment: What I do know is that I picked up her story like it was my own. And believing it felt safer than risking betrayal. But it didn't protect me; it just kept me secluded.

Rewrite it: I've been told that Gramma had a tough experience. And it may be true that *some* women *might* crush your spirit. But others will be your ride-or-die, the ones who hold you up when it matters most. I can name five of those kinds of ride-or-die women—my friends—right off the bat.

I would not have known them if I hadn't rewritten the script.

Or a more recent story: my "fluffy" narrative.

Name the source: I've looked in the mirror at my five-foot-nine, 175-pound, 53-year-old middle-aged body and compared it to my 42-year-old physique-competitor self. That younger body was lean and photo-ready, but it was also restless, making bargains with herself to outrun feelings she didn't want to face.

Test the alignment: So when I call myself "fluffy," logos pushes back: Am I being attuned, buoyant, and clear (remember ethos)? Am I honoring the body that has carried me this far? Why is "fluff" necessarily bad or shameful?

The rewrite: The body isn't the trophy. The life inside it is.

That's what logos does. It doesn't just correct the record. It shines a light on the stories you've inherited or rehearsed, even the ones whose origins you may never fully know, and teaches you how to reclaim authorship. Logos invites you to question, "Is that so?"

When the True Story Meets the Moment

As I wrote at the chapter's start, Jasmine once called news articles "stories." At the time, I corrected her. Now I see that she was pointing to something essential: Stories aren't just what we consume; they're what we live inside. Some we choose. Many we inherit. And left unexamined, they decide for us where the edges of possibility are.

That's why logos matters. It isn't just the "logic and reason" point of the Leadership Compass; it's the connective tissue.

The Leadership Compass as a whole reflects what's true. Logos gives it words.

Context shows us where we are. Logos arranges it into clarity.

Ethos reminds us of who we are and who we've chosen to be. Logos helps us articulate it.

Pathos reveals what we feel and value. Logos tests whether the bubbling story is worth believing, the value worth prioritizing.

Without logos, the Leadership Compass tilts off-balance. Logos is both flashlight and ledger; it illuminates and it accounts. With it, we audit the story, steady the mirror, and prepare for what's next.

Which brings us to the next anchor: exigence and kairos. Because once you know the story and can tell it with clarity, the question becomes: "Why now?"

Timing matters.

Urgency matters.

A true story, spoken at the right moment, can shift *everything*.

CHAPTER 8

When the Call Meets the Moment

Exigence Names the Demand.
Kairos Decides Its Time

There are words that cut without changing us. And there are words that arrive like medicine, not because they're kinder or smarter, but because they meet us at the exact moment we're ready to hear them.

I've lived both. Professors' comments that left me gutted but unchanged. A stranger's question over hot wings and Coronas that shifted my entire trajectory. Same kind of words—feedback, challenge, invitation—but only some of them stuck.

Why? Because some moments carry urgency, and some moments carry ripeness. It takes both for words to move from noise into turning point. The rhetoricians have a name for this pairing: exigence and kairos: the call and the time.

Our truest stories don't reveal themselves in one pass. They have to be turned over, reframed, revisited—until you can see the shape that's truer for who you are now. Exigence and kairos name why that turning becomes possible in the first place.

Professor Hat, One Last Time

Okay, last time I'm wearing my Professor Hat. I promise. (And if you don't believe me, well...Aristotle probably wouldn't either. He believed rhetoric was everywhere, so technically the hat never comes off. But let's not tell him that.)

Here's the quick frame: Aristotle said rhetoric was "the faculty of observing in any given case the available means of persuasion."[1] The "means," as you might recall, include ethos, pathos, and logos. Persuasion isn't magic. It's noticing what the moment demands, sensing whether the conditions are right to respond, and choosing a balanced mix of appeals.

Later, scholars broke rhetoric down into exigence, audience, and constraints. Through the *Lead Yourself First* lens, the audience isn't out there; it's in here. Inside each of us. We are both speaker and listener, persuader and persuaded. And the study doesn't happen in a pause outside of life; it happens in motion, in the middle of the moment.

Exigence names the demand or the call. Kairos decides the time. Constraints are the limits that hold us back. Together, they don't just prompt action; they invite revision, turning an old story through a new lens.

These elements don't live in neat boxes. They bleed into each other. What looks like exigence often carries pathos—

the decision to speak up in a meeting may be driven as much by frustration as by necessity. What looks like logos often reveals ethos—the data you choose to defend usually points to the kind of person you are. That's not a problem; it's the nature of real life. The point isn't to keep them separate, but to notice how each one can help us see a story more clearly.

Still too woo-woo and out there? Let me show you what I mean.

Words That Landed and Mirrors That Reflected

Let's revisit some of the stories I've already told you in this book and look at some other ones, too, to illustrate the point.

Kerry...And the Words That Broke Through

In Chapter 5, I told the story of walking into PYP Studio raw with grief, carrying more weight than I could name. In that season, Kerry, owner of and teacher at the studio, knelt above me at the close of a yoga class, brushed her fingers across my brow, and whispered, "You are whole. You are complete. Just as you are."

The exigence (demand or call) was obvious: I was cracked open, desperate for something to cut through the noise of loss. But exigence alone doesn't guarantee change. I had been told other things in that season—platitudes meant to comfort, condolences meant to soothe—and they passed right through me. Even though I felt "broken" at the time,

I was still "whole and complete," just as I was, but I was trapped by a guilt and grief story.

What made Kerry's words different—what made me finally see that I actually was "whole and complete"—was kairos (timing). In that moment, I was raw enough to hear the words, emptied out enough through the practice of yoga to let them in. If she had said them to me years earlier, I would've shrugged them off. If she had said them weeks later, I might have been too armored again to receive them. But in that exact moment, my own readiness met her gentle truth.

Exigence named the ache; kairos made the timing right. Without both, her words would've been just another kindness. With both, they became a turning point.

Javier… And the Question That Changed My Course

In 1995, I graduated from Penn State with a BA in English, but graduation didn't come with a handbook for what would come next. My passion was to be a writer and an editor. I had applied to nearly 50 publishing houses in New York City, and every envelope that came back postmarked from New York City was either a rejection or no envelope arrived at all; just silence.

So I drifted for the next several years. I picked up a bartending job to pay the bills, trading one kind of story for another—overhearing fragments of lives across the bar while wondering what to do with my own.

I had been told before that I lacked direction. Professors scrawled comments in red ink. Relatives offered backhanded advice about "getting my head out of the clouds." Those words hit hard, but they didn't move me. They kept me stuck.

That's where Javier walked into the story. Monday nights, 20 hot wings, three Coronas. At first, he was just a regular customer. Friendly. Kind. Often joined by his wife. Someone I could talk with easily, without pretense.

One night, after months of me drifting and Javier noticing, Javier looked at me, dead in the eye, and asked bluntly, "Liz, what are you going to do with the rest of your life?"

The exigence was already there: I was restless, unmoored, tired of drifting but unsure how to chart a course. But kairos was what made his words land. Javier wasn't a professor marking me down or a relative shaming me into obedience. He was an advisor in the College of Education, and more importantly, he was the first person connected with the university who seemed to actually give a damn about my future. I had spent my entire undergraduate years without mentorship—no advisor meetings, no professor stepping in, even though I made it abundantly clear I was in need of help and guidance. And here was someone, finally, who cared enough to ask.

Same question I'd been asked before, but in that moment, the soil was finally ready.

That conversation is how I found my way into graduate school. It's how I became a teacher, then professor. It's how I discovered that writing and teaching weren't competing paths, but intertwined ones. Looking back now, it wasn't just Javier's words that changed me. It was the timing. The need was real, and the time was ripe. That's the formula: The call was there all along, but it only became movement when ripeness met demand.

Same question, different moment, entirely new result.

Lifeboat Ethics…When Context Makes Silence Impossible

In Chapter 4 "Reading the Room," I described pushing back on an assignment called Lifeboat Ethics just months after 9/11. The assignment required me to ask students to rank who deserved to survive in a simulated Titanic-style disaster. On paper, it was framed as an exercise in reasoning. But in context, many of my students were from New York City. They were still shaken, grieving, raw.

The exigence was clear: Harm was baked into the assignment. Asking those students to decide who lives and who dies wasn't just provocative; it was cruel. But the kairos is what made it impossible to ignore. In another year, the assignment might have passed as "difficult but doable." In that moment, it was intolerable.

That's why I spoke up—not just privately, but publicly. The classroom container wasn't ready to hold the exercise, and silence would have meant complicity. Exigence pressed, kairos insisted, and I responded. In another context, the same assignment might have provoked a different reaction. But that day, with that audience, the demand and the timing aligned, and silence was no longer an option.

The Mirror Moments…When Paychecks Become Cages

Exigence and kairos have shown up in quieter places too. In Chapter 3 "Mirror, Mirror on the Wall," I wrote about my eventual decision to leave a consulting relationship where the paycheck felt like security but the environment was shrinking me. The exigence had been there for months: ideas buried under fear, proposals that stalled unless they came spreadsheet-ready, an undertow of hesitation masked as diligence.

But the kairos didn't come until I admitted the paycheck was costing me more than it paid. Only then did I act. Clarity was there all along, but urgency and timing had to converge before I could move.

Your Turn

Exigence and kairos aren't just abstract Greek terms; they're part of the Leadership Compass we've been building all along. They ask us to orient ourselves in time and demand:

- What's calling for a response right now?
- Is this the right moment to act?
- Am I rushing, delaying, or attuned?

Logos might test a story's truth, but exigence and kairos decide whether it becomes ours to live. They remind us that leadership without them is just noise. With them, words become turning points.

I know, because I've carried old tapes that only shifted when demand and timing finally aligned. For years, I lived under: "I need a job to keep this roof over my head, to pay the bills, and to avoid being a burden." That story constrained me until kairos ripened, and I realized I could build a financial runway, not just survive. I carried "lacks focus and direction" like a wound until exigence demanded I see the direction already built into my habits, health anchors, and future plans. "Rejection" letters? No. Think of them instead as "not the right fit right now" letters.

I've seen it play out in larger ways, too. When Jeff died, people expected a long season of mourning. They didn't know how abusive he'd been, how much of myself I'd already lost long before he was gone. I felt the grief, but I also felt release, a timing I didn't ask for but couldn't ignore. The demand and the moment aligned. Exigence said, "It's time to live differently." Kairos said, "Now."

Your stories will look different. Exigence might sound like your body forcing you to rest—maybe through burnout or an illness you can't ignore—or like a relationship fraying under strain. Kairos might look like an opportunity you weren't ready for last year but suddenly feels possible now. The details change, but the pattern is the same: demand + timing = turning point.

Because when the call is real and the time is ripe, words and stories don't just sound good. They change you. And sometimes, that change takes more than one telling. A single story might need to be turned—once, twice, even three times—before it reveals the version that's true enough to carry forward.

That's where we'll go next. Part 3 offers one more piece: a tying together of all the loose ends and a compass for what to do from here.

PART 3
Leading from Wholeness

There comes a point when you stop needing every answer and start trusting yourself. The Leadership Compass isn't something you hold anymore. It lives in you. What began as awareness has become embodiment, a quiet rhythm that steadies your steps even when the path is uncertain. When you become practiced at letting the Leadership Compass anchor you, it transforms into your internal GPS: a way of moving through the world unobstructed, whole, and free. This is where clarity becomes leadership; where coming home to yourself becomes not just an arrival, but a way of being.

CHAPTER 9

The Way Forward

How the Compass Turns into Your Internal GPS

When we started out with Chapters 1 and 2, I wasn't offering a plan. I was offering a mirror, really—something to help you see who you already are, not just who you thought you should be. Those chapters remind us that clarity doesn't come from chasing harder; it begins by stepping away from striving and returning to ourselves.

And it wasn't long before the mirror changed from compact to full-length, when we stepped before it to see our full selves in "Mirror, Mirror on the Wall." There, we traced the Leadership Compass in its entirety—its five points: context, ethos, pathos, logos, exigence, and kairos. Each one offers a way of anchoring yourself when the map goes blank, when the noise gets loud, when clarity feels just out of reach.

Since then, we've traveled anchor by anchor—never as a checklist, but as a way of finding our bearings. Each chapter, a turn of the needle. Each story, a reminder that leadership begins with the willingness to lead yourself first.

Now we arrive at the coalescence. Not the end, but the weaving together. The moment when the Leadership Compass stops being something you pick up and starts becoming something you carry within you.

This is The Way Forward.

What's In a Name?

For me, the first step in carrying the Leadership Compass inward was simple but foundational: I started with my name. Elizabeth Ann Holtzinger. A string of syllables chosen by my parents, wrapped in their reasons, carrying a heritage I didn't choose but inherited all the same.

I began to ask: "Why this name? What did it mean to them? What has it come to mean to me? And most importantly: Do I want to keep living by this story or choose another way?"

That practice opened a door. It showed me that before we can rewrite the larger stories of our lives, we begin with the ones we were handed. Names, roles, scripts—each of them offers a chance to ask whether we will continue to carry them or whether it's time to lay them down.

That's where I invite you to begin. Write the story of your name. Trace what you were given. Notice what you've carried. Decide what you want to keep and what you're ready to release.

What You Carry Now and Questions to Keep Turning

From there, return to the Leadership Compass. Each point carries forward what we practiced together:

- *The Way Back* → You know how to come home to yourself, to return to clarity, safety, and joy without having to earn it. *Your Turn:* Where in your life are you still trying to "earn" what's already yours?

- *Mirror, Mirror on the Wall* → You no longer need another map; the Leadership Compass shows you who you already are and what's true beneath the noise. *Your Turn:* When doubt creeps in, what mirror will you hold up to remind yourself of what's true?

- *Reading the Room* → You can recognize the layers of context—systemic, situational, and self—and sense whether the space you're in can actually hold your clarity. *Your Turn:* What room are you in, and can it metabolize the clarity you bring?

- *Who Are You Without the Title* → You lead from coherence, not title, grounding your ethos in the qualities that reflect who you most want to be. *Your Turn:* Who are you when the scaffolding of roles and titles falls away? More importantly, who do you want to be?

- *What Moves You (And What Shouldn't)* → You treat emotions as signals, not commands, creating space before you act so your choices align with what matters most. *Your Turn:* Which emotions deserve your energy, and which ones can you let pass?

- *The Stories That Sound Like Truth* → You can hold your stories up to the light, testing which still fit and which you're ready to rewrite or release. *Your Turn:* What story sounds true right now, and does it still deserve to lead?

- *When the Call Meets the Moment* → You can recognize when urgency and timing converge and trust yourself to act when the moment is ripe. *Your Turn:* What call is pressing on you now, and is this the moment to respond?

The Leadership Compass Becomes Your GPS

The Leadership Compass was never meant to be mastered like a subject in school. It was meant to be practiced, lived, trusted. The more you return to it—question by question, story by story—the more it becomes part of how you move through the world.

Over time, it shifts. The Leadership Compass becomes less an external tool and more an instinct. Less something you hold in your hand and more an orientation that lives within you. That's the mark of mastery: When the compass becomes your internal GPS—steady, sure, already inside you.

And once you've tuned it for yourself, you may notice it working outward, too. A presentation that doesn't land, a message that feels out of step, a conversation that falls flat—the same compass that helped you lead yourself first can help you recalibrate how you lead and connect with others.

Your GPS is already there, reminding you that you carry direction within you.

So take the first step. Tell the story of your name. Then tell the stories that follow. One turn at a time. One story at a time. Until the story you're living is no longer the one that held you back, but the one that carries you forward.

Forward only works when it's honest. The next step isn't about doing more. It's about reading your own story clearly enough to know which parts to carry and which ones to finally set down.

CHAPTER 10

Reading Your Own Story

How to Analyze the Persuasive Patterns That Shape Your Life

When we reach the end of a book, it can feel like we've arrived. But this kind of work—the work of leading yourself first—isn't a single arrival. It's a loop. A turning. A continual rereading of the stories that brought you here and the ones that will carry you forward.

If the Leadership Compass is a tool for orientation, then this final practice is a tool for interpretation. It helps you see not just where you are, but how your story has been speaking all along.

In my English 15 courses, I teach students to perform an analysis—to study how a text works on its audience: how it persuades, moves, or fails to move. Here, I want you to do something similar. Only this time, the "text" isn't an article or an ad. It's your life. And the audience you're analyzing isn't out there. It's you. You're the one who's been persuaded by this story all along.

The stories we tell about ourselves shape everything: how we decide, how we show up, and how we lead. If a story convinces you that you're small, you'll make safe choices. If it tells you that you're the only one who can hold everything together, you'll keep over-functioning long after it's healthy. These inherited narratives don't just live in our heads; they leak into our leadership. They influence how we listen, how we respond, and whether we trust others to carry their share.

So before you can lead others clearly, you have to understand the language of your own life—the *persuasive patterns* that have been shaping your choices all along. That's what this final exercise is about: stepping back to analyze the story you've been leading with, so you can decide whether it still fits the life—and the leadership—you want to live.

How to Analyze Your Life Story

1. Identify the Text

Name the story you've been living. Maybe it's "The One Who Always Shows Up" or "The One Who Keeps the Peace." Write a short summary—what happens, what it means, what it costs.

2. Name the Narrator

That's you, but which version? The achiever? The survivor? The caretaker? The skeptic? Each role writes with its own voice. Recognizing who's speaking helps you see the perspective that's been steering the story.

3. Define the Audience

Who was this story trying to reach or please? A parent, a partner, a boss, a crowd of invisible critics? Every story has an intended audience. Identifying it helps you see where you may have outsourced your clarity and reminds you that the audience that matters most is still you.

4. Clarify the Purpose

Ask: "What has this story been doing for me? Has it been protecting me, proving something, keeping me safe—or keeping me small?" Every narrative has a function, but not all of them still serve who you're becoming.

5. Examine the Appeals

Every story relies on credibility, emotion, and logic—on *ethos, pathos,* and *logos.*

- Ethos: Where does your credibility in this story come from?

- Pathos: Which emotions in this story drive your decisions or silence them?

- Logos: What reasoning in this story keeps the story intact?

Now zoom out. How has *context* shaped this story? What was the *kairos*—the moment, the timing—that made it make sense then, but maybe not now?

6. Evaluate the Fit

When I teach analysis, I ask whether a text offers a *fitting response* to its moment. Ask yourself the same question: "Is the story I've been telling still a fitting response to my life as it is today?"

7. Write Your Thesis

Every analysis arrives at a claim. Yours might sound like:

- *The story I've been living is no longer the story I believe.*

- *This story still fits, but I'm ready to tell it with more truth and less fear.*

- *It's time for a new draft.*

You don't have to share this with anyone. You just have to tell the truth—to yourself.

When I look back at the stories I've told throughout this book—the woman learning to separate love from obligation, the teacher finding confidence in her own words, the leader realizing that wholeness, not perfection, is what steadies a team—I can see how each version of me was searching for alignment. Every rupture, every return, every reframed story was practice for this kind of clarity. The Leadership Compass keeps you steady when everything else shifts. It reminds you that the answers aren't out there; they live inside the story you're already telling.

And that's the point of leading yourself first—not to arrive somewhere new, but to recognize where you are, to read your own story with honesty, and to come home to yourself, again and again.

Returning to the Work

You won't do this once and be done with it. The work of self-leadership is iterative. You'll circle back to these same stories, sometimes years later, and see them differently. You'll notice new audiences, new motives, new meanings. You'll reframe what once hurt, recontextualize what once defined you, and reclaim what still matters.

If these ideas resonate with you, I'd love to keep the conversation going. You can find me on *Unfold,* my Substack publication (https://lholtzinger.substack.com/), where I write about living the Leadership Compass in real life— through the lenses of travel, relationship, body, and work. It's where this framework continues to unfold in practice, one story at a time.

EPILOGUE

The Turn Home

There will be days when you forget everything you've read here. You'll fall back into old stories, reach for the familiar map, and try to muscle your way toward clarity again. You'll look for answers in the same places that once failed to hold them. And when that happens—because it will—remember this: Forgetting isn't failure. It's part of the work. We don't stay clear. We *return* to clarity.

We lose the thread, so we can learn to trace it again, more gently this time.

That's what *Lead Yourself First* has always been about—not the permanent state of being self-led, but the willingness to notice when you've drifted and to find your way back. Leadership, at its core, is reorientation. It's waking up, mid-story, and realizing you've been persuaded by an old script that no longer fits. And then choosing—quietly, deliberately—to write a truer one.

If you've done this work with me, you already know it doesn't stop at the page. The compass doesn't live in theory; it lives in your day-to-day turns. Every choice, every silence, every "not yet" moment is another chance to lead yourself toward what's true.

You'll do this work again and again, because life will keep giving you new drafts—new characters, new scenes, new stakes. Each one will ask something different of you: more courage here, more grace there. The persuasive patterns that once kept you safe will try to step forward again. They'll whisper, "This is who you are."

That's when you pause, listen, and test the story: "Is it true now? Does it still serve? Or is it time to turn the page?"

This practice doesn't end. It evolves.

You'll revisit the same stories from new vantage points— the younger self who lived them, the present self who is interpreting them, the future self who is healing them. You'll turn them over, like stones in your hand, feeling how they've smoothed with time.

That's what this next season of the work invites you into: the ongoing practice of returning to yourself through reflection, writing, and lived experience. It's what I write about on *Unfold,* my Substack publication (https:// lholtzinger.substack.com/): the Leadership Compass in motion through travel, relationship, work, and the body. Because the work doesn't end. It deepens.

Each time you come back to your story, you'll find something new: a truth you couldn't face before, a grace you couldn't yet hold, a peace that was waiting for you beneath the noise.

You'll remember that leadership isn't about control or certainty. It's about presence. And that the compass you've been consulting all along was never really a tool at all. It was your life, asking to be listened to.

So when you lose your way again, don't panic. Look for the signs you already know:

- The pulse of stillness beneath the noise.
- The tug of alignment when something rings true.
- The quiet conviction that says: "Here. This way."

That's your compass speaking.

That's you, leading yourself home.

NOTES

Chapter 1

1. Adam Grant, *Granted* (Substack), May 19, 2025, https://open.substack.com/users/7011567-adam-grant?utm_source=mentions.

Chapter 4

1. William A. Covino and David A. Jolliffe, "What Is Rhetoric?," in *Rhetoric: Concepts, Definitions, Boundaries*, ed. William A. Covino and David A. Jolliffe (Boston: Allyn & Bacon, 1995), 1–13.

2. Covino and Jolliffe, "What Is Rhetoric?," 10.

3. Jean M. Twenge, *Generations: The Real Differences Between Gen Z, Millennials, Gen X, Boomers, and Silents—and What They Mean for America's Future* (New York: Atria Books, 2023).

Chapter 5

1. Harris III, *The Wonder Switch: The Difference Between Limiting Your Life and Living Your Dream* (Nashville: W Publishing, an imprint of Thomas Nelson, 2020).

2. Kerry Bestwick (@kerrybestwick), Instagram (accessed November 5, 2025), https://www.instagram.com/kerrybestwick/.

3.   Daniel H. Pink, *To Sell Is Human: The Surprising Truth About Moving Others* (New York: Riverhead Books, 2012).

Chapter 7

1.   Lee Honeycutt, "Aristotle's Rhetoric, Book 1, Chapter 2," in *Stasis Theory: A Webtext on Rhetoric and Argument*, Kairos: A Journal of Rhetoric, Technology, and Pedagogy, 2017, https://kairos.technorhetoric.net/stasis/2017/honeycutt/aristotle/rhet1-2.html.

2.   Michael McRay, "StoryOS," Istoria Institute (accessed November 5, 2025), https://istoria.com/storyos/.

Chapter 8

1.   Aristotle, *Rhetoric*, trans. W. Rhys Roberts, Book 1, chap. 2, in Lee Honeycutt, "Stasis Theory: A Webtext on Rhetoric and Argument," Kairos: A Journal of Rhetoric, Technology, and Pedagogy, 2017, https://kairos.technorhetoric.net/stasis/2017/honeycutt/aristotle/rhet1-2.html.

ACKNOWLEDGMENTS

First and foremost, I thank God—and Jesus Christ, my Lord and Savior—who has been with me through all of it. Who walked with me, beside me, and carried me through the pain. Who delivered me from evil. Who never left me, never forsook me, and always loved me. No matter what.

To my parents, Albert J. Holtzinger II and Rita Heikes Holtzinger, who have always known who I was, even when I couldn't see myself. And to my sister, Jennifer Holtzinger Bates, who gave me tough love when I needed it most and a bed to sleep in when I had nowhere else to go.

To my friends who became lifelines: Tricia Turner, who has known me since college and saw everything; Amy Powell, who took me by the hand to yoga and fed me when I wanted to waste away; and Kerry Bestwick, who held me in her lap when I broke and stood beside me when I was ready to march forward.

To Bethanne Zimmerman, former therapist and now dear friend, who helps me make up stories that make us laugh like the old ladies we swear we're not.

And to GMFW, the man who loves me without condition or performance, who met me where I was and never asked me to be anything other than myself. The one whose presence quieted the noise, whose steadiness reminded me that love can be simple, safe, and true. You are the answer to prayers I didn't know how to pray.

To Nancy Pile, my editor, who helped me refine what I was still trying to say and gave my thoughts the clarity they were asking for. You saw what this book wanted to become before I did, and you helped me lead it home. In the process, you showed me that this work—*this way of leading ourselves first*—works. Watching you let the book do its work on you reminded me why I wrote it in the first place.

To my colleagues and friends at Penn State, thank you for being part of the better story. While pain once lived here, it doesn't anymore. What remains is purpose, partnership, and the grace to keep doing meaningful work alongside people I deeply respect.

And finally, to everyone who's reading, listening, and pausing to ask the hard questions with me. My hope is that these pages gave you a language for what you've always known but maybe hadn't yet named: that clarity, courage, and belonging start within.

A Quick Ask!

Thank you for reading this book. If it met you
where you needed it, I'd be grateful if you'd
take a moment to share your thoughts.

Your review helps this work find the people who need
it next — and it guides what future books become.

If you have two minutes, you can leave a review
on Amazon and let me know what stayed with
you, what shifted, or what made you think.

Be Well,

Liz

ABOUT THE AUTHOR

Liz Holtzinger is a professor, writer, and storyteller who has spent most of her life paying close attention—to people, to language, and to the quiet turning points we often don't notice until we look back. After more than two decades teaching rhetoric and writing at the university level, and years building and leading organizations beyond it, she finally stopped dodging her own voice and started writing the stories she'd been carrying for years.

Now she splits her time between the page and the microphone, exploring what it means to live by a compass you actually trust. Her work shows up everywhere she does: in classrooms and leadership conversations, in airports, on long walks, in moments of transition, and on *Unfold*, her digital magazine where clarity tends to sneak up on her mid-sentence.

She writes about alignment, courage, the body, work, and the strange and wonderful ways clarity reshapes how we live, decide, and lead when we stop performing and start paying attention. No longer contorting herself to fit institutions, roles, or expectations, her work reflects the freedom—and authority—of someone who has led, built, and let go.

She also believes in good coffee, well-timed exits, and the kind of laughter that tells the truth.

Liz lives freely now, and her writing invites readers to do the same.

CONTINUING THE CONVERSATION

If this book stirred something in you, there's more to explore. *Unfold* is where the work continues in real time—through essays about travel, relationship, the body, and the everyday moments that test (and reveal) our alignment. It's where the Leadership Compass shows up off the page and inside a lived life.

You can subscribe at **lholtzinger.substack.com** to follow along as the ideas evolve, deepen, and take new shapes—one story at a time.

Stay Connected

If this book met you at an important moment, you're welcome to stay connected in the social places where the work continues to unfold.

You can find more writing, reflections, and behind-the-scenes notes here:

Instagram: @liz.holtzinger
LinkedIn: linkedin.com/in/elizabethholtzinger

Speaking & Events

For organizations, teams, and leaders navigating moments of transition, complexity, or change, I offer keynote talks and spoken-word narrative experiences. Each engagement weaves story, reflection, and lived practice to clarify how decisions are made, how culture is shaped, and how people lead themselves—and others—inside real systems. The result is not performance for its own sake, but language and perspective audiences can carry back into their work.

To inquire about availability, visit:
lizholtzinger.com

www.ingramcontent.com/pod-product-compliance
Lightning Source LLC
Chambersburg PA
CBHW071603120726
47973CB00053B/276/J